FASHION VISIONARIES

LINDA WATSON

LAURENCE KING

Published in 2015 by
Laurence King Publishing Ltd
361–373 City Road
London EC1V 1LR
e-mail: enquiries@laurenceking.com
www.laurenceking.com

A catalogue record for this book is available from the
British Library.

ISBN: 978 1 78067 578 7

Printed in China

Book Design: TwoSheds Design
Cover Design: Alexandre Coco, from an original concept
by Pentagram; lettering by Jason Brooks
Cover Image: Chanel wearing one of her designs, 1937.
© Horst P. Horst/Condé Nast Publications
Senior Editor: Melissa Danny
Picture Researcher: Heather Vickers

FASHION VISIONARIES

LINDA WATSON

Laurence King Publishing

FASHION
VISIONARIES

Introduction

The progressions, inventions, and seismic changes in fashion have taken many forms, and the visionary designers featured in this book are equally eclectic: elegant, outrageous, urbane, eccentric. From revolutionaries to revisionists, provocateurs to aesthetes, in each case their creative output has defined their identity and, ultimately, altered the way we dress. Together they have provided the most memorable fashion moments of modern times. The way they have delivered them has been as diverse as their design ideas.

In fashion, timing is everything. There have been temporary moments of madness, seasons of conformity, years where a particular colour has dominated the landscape, a decade that could be summed up by a single item of clothing. The fascination of fashion has always been its mercurial nature, and the element of surprise is essential. These visionaries have shaken up the fashion world, be it with a radical reworking of proportion, a surprising take on fabrication, an unexpected sartorial combination, or the ingenious redrawing of a silhouette. The subtleties and the shocks are equally relevant and both can have an indelible impact. Landmark happenings – epitomized by Dior's New Look – seemingly arrive out of nowhere and take the fashion world by storm. With the advantage of hindsight they came to fruition at precisely the right time. Contrary to popular belief, these ideas are not simply a result of divine inspiration, but often a direct reflection of social revolution. The mini, for example, would not have occurred without the advent of the Swinging Sixties, where the abbreviated hemline and air of youthful rebellion worked hand in hand.

Unlike many design disciplines that rely on observation, fashion is completely interactive. It always has the human figure to consider. At its core is an immovable template: the anatomy in motion. Sitting, standing, walking, turning, running are just some of the human manoeuvres that inevitably put a different perspective on a particular silhouette or proportion. Fashion works best when it flatters, but some of the most radical ideas have had the opposite effect. Some designers have exposed parts of the body usually kept under cover, treading a fine line between revealing and concealing – one of the trickiest talents to master. A chosen few have perfected this to a fine art.

The world of fashion is composed of historians and futurists – those who analyze what has gone before, and those who are focused resolutely on the new. Whether they look backwards or forwards, all visionary designers have a common denominator: the ability to make a definitive decision. For those whose life's work centres on style, making a statement is second nature. Their unique design signature – be it understated or extreme – must not only be consistent, but also continually desirable. Success is often a consequence of perennial reinvention. Consider the case of Chanel and her classic tweed suit, which is still the epitome of modernity despite existing for over half a century. For the consumer, fashion pivots on a handful of key points: culture, climate, identity, sexuality. Occasion is important, but the most telling point is the wearer's personality. Nothing reveals more about a person's mood, attitude, approach to life and inner thoughts than the clothes they wear.

The twenty-first-century fashion designer is no longer concerned solely with sartorial matters. Not only do designers need to apply their vision to a variety of market levels – often from couture's inner sanctum to the relative accessibility of diffusion lines – but to developing their brand across a wide spectrum of products including perfume, handbags, shoes and pillowcases. Among the visionary designers featured in this book are the visionary brand-makers. Some of the world's most covetable, instantly identifiable labels were a consequence of instinct, often stemming from spotting a gap in the market and producing a prototype, to which the public responded. In many cases that initial idea has changed very little since its conception. Little did they know, years later, that their seed of an idea would turn into a fashion phenomenon worth billions of dollars. The global popularity of some of fashion's most visionary brands is breathtaking. Even more amazing is the way they have retained their kudos. Within this book there are those revolutionary fashion designers who have completely changed the course of fashion history. The vast majority, however, are simply original thinkers who have made an indelible mark.

'We have an unerring
commitment to quality
and craftsmanship.'

Thierry Hermès

1801–1878

GERMANY

One of the oldest and most revered of French brands, Hermès is a byword for unashamed luxury, famed around the world for its high-quality leather goods and high-fashion accessories. Originally a saddler to the aristocracy of Europe, Hermès introduced handbags and clothing after almost a hundred years in business; it took precisely a century to launch the product for which it would become globally synonymous: silk scarves.

The founder was Thierry Hermès, who was born in Krefeld, Germany, but the family moved to France in 1828. In 1837 Thierry established a harness-making shop in Paris, where Napoleon III and Empress Eugénie were early customers. The founder's son, Charles-Émile Hermès, expanded the line in late 1879. Now manufacturing saddles, a new Hermès branch opened at 24 rue du Faubourg Saint-Honoré, where the flagship store remains today.

By 1914, as many as 80 saddle craftsmen were employed in the business. A pioneering company, Hermès was the first to secure exclusive rights to introduce the zip fastener in France, where it was renamed the Hermès fastener. During the 1920s an accessory collection was created, and then clothing was introduced. The 1950s were a turning point for Hermès, as the Kelly bag (then known as the 'Sac à dépêches') gained worldwide attention after it was adopted by actress Grace Kelly, who had discovered it on a Paris shopping trip. The second Hermès classic, the Birkin bag, was the result of a chance meeting between actress and singer Jane Birkin and then-Hermès boss Jean-Louis Dumas on a transatlantic flight in 1981.

Hermès retains its original values and rejects any suggestion of mass production; the majority of its products are made in France by craftspeople, often a single artisan carrying out the entire process. Known for making classic accessories rather than cutting-edge fashion, the Hermès range now includes everything from scarves to tableware. The famous silk scarf, first introduced in 1937 to celebrate the company's centenary, is still manufactured in the same way, being individually screen-printed and hemmed by hand. There have been more than 2,000 designs since production began, and it is claimed that an Hermès scarf is sold somewhere in the world every 25 seconds.

Hermès is as famous for its handmade leather goods as for its scarves. A single handbag can take up to 24 hours to produce and signature bags often have at least a six-month waiting list. In 2004 a Birkin bag made of crocodile, gold and diamonds and costing $81,000 was produced to celebrate this cult bag's twentieth anniversary.

The Hermès clothing collection has had two high-profile designers at the helm: Martin Margiela (1997–2003; p. 261) and Jean Paul Gaultier (2003–10; p. 249). When Gaultier departed from Hermès he called it 'a love story. Like all love stories it had to end'.

Opposite Refined, streamlined plaid coat with godet panels, flared cuffed sleeves, cinched waist and chic co-ordinating accessories. 1952.

Gaultier takes the classic equestrian elements – dressage hat, facial veiling, leather accessories – and pairs it with the subtlety of chiffon drapery. 2004.

Thierry Hermès

1801 Born in Krefeld, Germany (then Prussia)

1810

1820

1828 Hermès family move to France

1830 Opens first harness shop in Paris

1837

1840

1850

1855 Wins first prize in his category at the Exposition Universelle, Paris

1860

1870

1878 Dies and the company is taken over by his sons Charles-Émile and Adolphe

Brand

1880 Flagship store founded

1900 The Haut à Courroies' bag is created

1922 First leather bag created with patented zipper

1929 First women's couture collection previewed in Paris

1937 Creation and introduction of Hermès silk scarves

HERMÈS
SELLIER
24, Fᴳ Sᵗ HONORÉ PARIS

MAROQUINERIE
VOYAGES - SPORTS
■

| ALGER | CANNES | PAU - Sᵗ CYR |
| BIARRITZ | CHANTILLY | SAUMUR |

Bringing the brand to the fore in an effective advertisement that illustrates a golfing swing, underlining the company's sporting angle. 1929.

BIARRITZ · CANNES · DEAUVILLE · LILLE · MONTE-CARLO

Top Classic advertising featuring the three key accessories – Kelly bag, signature print scarf and pair of elegant leather gloves.

Above Grace Kelly and Prince Rainier in a paparazzi shot in 1956 that propelled this bag, re-christened the 'Kelly', to

La Grande Dame #14

Soc. de Publ. d'Art

Toilette de Soirée
Modèle de Worth

Dillon

2. 1894

'Clothes have a great deal
to do with one's happiness.'

Charles Frederick Worth

1825–1895

UNITED KINGDOM

Credited with being the founder of haute couture, Charles Frederick Worth introduced a series of revolutionary firsts. He was the first to show garments on live mannequins and the first to sign his work with a label. His ingenious idea – that dresses should be presented as a finished entity as opposed to individual commissions – was to change the course of couture. Previously socialites, not dressmakers, had set the tone of fashion. The *New York Times* described Worth as 'one of the most powerful personages of our epoch'.

With little formal education, Worth taught himself about culture, spending every spare moment studying the great paintings in museums and art galleries. Moving from London to Paris in 1845, he began working in a small dry-goods store, from where he progressed to Maison Gagelin, a house that sold cashmere shawls, fabrics and ready-made coats. This was where Worth began to revolutionize fashion.

Worth married the house model, Marie Vernet. As an accomplished and extremely persuasive salesman, he started to design gowns for her, leading to his being invited to open a department dedicated solely to dressmaking. This was the forerunner to the modern couturier's atelier, where buyers were invited to inspect the current collection. With his designs evocative of a bygone era, Worth's talent was spotted by the ladies of the court of Napoleon III.

When Worth was turned down for a partnership in Maison Gagelin, he decided to start his own business. In 1858, together with the Swedish businessman Otto

Bobergh, he opened Worth & Bobergh at 7 rue de la Paix. By 1871, the new House of Worth had 1,200 people in his employ, his reputation had reached America and *Harper's Bazaar* was writing reviews of his salon. One customer stated: 'What doesn't show is as good as what does, so that when the right side is quite worn out I shall simply wear the wrong side.' His most high-profile client, Empress Eugénie, called him '*le tyran de la mode*'.

His gowns, which cost as much as $10,000, were owned by American society names such as the Carnegies, the Rockefellers, the Vanderbilts and the Astors. Russian aristocracy, whose extravagant tastes were legendary, also made up a large proportion of Worth's clientele. Worth was even reputed to have been responsible for the invention of the bustle.

When Worth died in 1895, *Harper's Bazaar* waxed lyrical: 'No painter, no sculptor, no poet, no actor, no novelist of the past three decades has achieved so widespread a fame as that of this dressmaker of the rue de la Paix.'

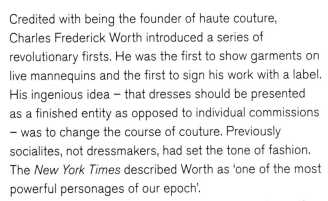

Opposite Decorative detailing on the sleeve head and voluminous drapery across the torso attract attention to the décolletage. 1894.

Charles Frederick Worth

Born in Bourne, England

Works as a book keeper for Swan and Edgar before moving to Lewis and Allenby

Relocates to Paris; employed by Maison Gagelin

Marries his muse, Marie Vernet, and contributes prize-winning designs displayed in the Great Exhibition, London

Worth's court train dress is exhibited in the Exposition Universelle, Paris

Otto Bobergh finances the establishment Worth & Bobergh

Salon re-opens as House of Worth and customers now include the Empress of France

1820   1825   1830   1838 1840   1845   18 1851   1855   1858 1860   18 1871

Opposite Lavishly embroidered evening dress, with foliage designed to accentuate the seamlines and extended train. 1896.

Top Powder pink, silk satin boned corset with criss-cross sequinned decoration, and delicate lace sleeves dotted with rosebuds. 1890.

Right Using precisely striped plain and jacquard fabric, and a row of satin-covered buttons, the hourglass silhouette is defined. 1884.

Dies in Paris, France

· · · · · · · · · · 1890 · · · · · 1895 · · · · 1900 · · · · · · · · · · 1910 · · · · · · · · · · 1920 · · · · · · · · · · 1930 · · · · · · · · · 1940

'Style never means conspicuousness.'

Thomas Burberry

1835–1926

UNITED KINGDOM

Equal parts innovator and inventor, Thomas Burberry had a revolutionary sartorial vision that was rooted in sportswear. As a consequence of his ability to observe human nature, understand longevity, appreciate necessity and align it with business acumen, he unwittingly became the founder of one of the most profitable brands on the planet. Although the label is now synonymous with trench coats, a signature check and quintessential Britishness, the Burberry ethos was based on the formulation of one of the world's first performance fabrics.

Burberry made his name by creating and patenting a material he called gabardine. Lightweight, durable, breathable and encompassing all the properties associated with the most enduring textiles, in a world populated by heavy, inflexible outdoor materials, it was a revelation. Few fashion statements are still as relevant a century after their creation, but the Burberry raincoat, subject to numerous fashionable incarnations, remains the brand's international bestseller.

Born into the farming community in the county of Surrey, Burberry served his apprenticeship at a local draper's shop before opening his own clothing outfitters at 21 years old, in Basingstoke. His store was frequented by customers who took part in traditional English country pursuits – fishing, foxhunting, horseriding – and it was the sporting passions of the local people that were the inspiration for the collection. Burberry's aim was to create a line of clothing that not only appealed aesthetically, but more importantly, was adapted to a temperamental climate and fulfilled the demands of country life. In 1888 Burberry patented gabardine, going on to sell it wholesale. By 1891, the company had grown to the extent that it relocated to central London. A decade later, Burberry had made sufficient impact on an international scale that a Paris branch was opened.

In the same way that celebrities were to become an integral part of Burberry's twenty-first-century success, in the company's early days it was endorsement from explorers that underlined the Burberry brand. In 1897, Major F. G. Jackson, famed for mapping parts of the Arctic Circle, wore Burberry. Celebrated aviator Claude Grahame-White donned Burberry attire when he became the first person to fly between London and Manchester in less than 24 hours. The most famous link was Roald Amundsen, who in 1911 became the first person to reach the South Pole. After the global impact of the Antarctic expedition, Burberry created the predecessor to what would become a classic – the trench coat. Called the 'Tielocken coat', it featured a single strap, buckle fastening and button at the collar, and enjoyed great popularity with army officers during World War I. In 1912, Burberry made and supplied the gabardine tent that accompanied Robert Scott on his attempt to reach the South Pole wearing Burberry. The Burberry identity was established. During the 1930s the company branched into winter sports outfits. Today, the essential Burberry ingredients remain intact.

Opposite The trench is restyled for the twenty-first century with subtle changes in proportion and the addition of fur edging. 2006.

Thomas Burberry

Born in Brockham Green, England

Burberry brand is founded

1820		1830	1835	1840		1850	1856	1860		1870		

For Winter Sports, Burberry provides the most protective and comfortable dress. Designed in consultation with experts, Burberry models embody the essentials for full enjoyment of sport on snow or ice.

Burberry Winter Sports materials — dense textures — lightweights — smooth surfaces — Burberry-proofed — snow will not lodge to congeal or penetrate, cold winds will not chill or hot sun overheat.

Winter Sports Catalogue and Patterns of Materials Post Free

BURBERRYS HAYMARKET LONDON S.W. 1
BD. MALESHERBES PARIS & AGENTS

Opposite With minor differences between the male and female versions, this classically cut trench coat, c. 1930, has adhered to the same template for decades.

Left The renewed emphasis on winter sports in the mid 1920s required a revolutionary wardrobe of technological textile advances and lightweight fabrics.

Below left The signature check, originally present in the trench coat lining, is translated into a zipped gilet for Autumn/Winter 2001.

Below Since the intervention of American retail supremo Rose Marie Bravo in the mid 1990s, Burberry has enjoyed phenomenal global success.

Company opens first London store at No. 30 Haymarket

Major F. G. Jackson is photographed wearing Burberry

Roald Amundsen reached the South Pole wearing Burberry

The Tielocken coat (trench coat) is patented

Burberry's new store opens at No. 18–21 Haymarket, designed by architect Walter Cave

Retires to Abbots Court, Dorset

Dies in Hook, England

1891 **1897** 1900 **1911** **1912** **1913** **1917** 1920 **1926** 1930 1940

'Fashion is not always about what's new. It's also about what's good.'

Jeanne Lanvin

1867–1946

FRANCE

The oldest French fashion house still in existence was founded by an incurable romantic called Jeanne Lanvin. 'I act on impulse and believe in instinct,' she said in 1934. 'My dresses aren't premeditated. I am carried away by feeling and technical knowledge helps me make my clothes become a reality.' The Lanvin signatures of subtlety and femininity were underlined by inventive embellishment. Delicate embroideries, ruffles, appliqués, quilting, velvet flowers, lace rosettes and free-flowing ribbons in a palette of pretty shades were a few of the many decorative effects Lanvin deployed. Called the 'fairy godmother of the *jeune fille*', she deftly combined sophisticated fabrics with an air of youthful refinement.

At 13 years old, Lanvin underwent a dressmaking apprenticeship at the House of Talbot before training in millinery techniques at Madame Félix. The financial investment of a wealthy client enabled Lanvin to establish her own millinery workshop, but it was clothes designed for her daughter that became the catalyst for a new business venture. Prompted by requests from admirers, Lanvin made adult versions of the infant outfits, creating a collection that captured both the women's and the girls' markets.

The multitalented Lanvin discovered she was just as at ease creating elegant interiors as she was in the sphere of fashion and in 1920 she expanded her business to include Lanvin Décoration. A year after the opening, Lanvin was commissioned to collaborate with Armand-Albert Rateau on the interior decoration of the Théâtre Daunou in Paris. The 1920s were an era of diversification and empire-building for the House of Lanvin. Receiving increasing press coverage and refusing to rest on her laurels, she introduced bathing suits, sportswear, leisurewear, menswear, furs and lingerie. A dye factory was established in Nanterre to produce a specialist colour spectrum, in particular a shade of cornflower blue later christened Lanvin Blue. Exquisite shades inspired by a Fra Angelico fresco in Florence became a key signature in the Lanvin look. Her clientele straddled the worlds of celebrity and royalty, with the queens of Italy and Romania wearing Lanvin, in addition to cinematic stars Marlene Dietrich and Mary Pickford.

In recognition of her achievements, in 1926 Lanvin became the first female couturier to be named a Chevalier de la Légion d'Honneur, and in 1938 was elevated to Officier de la Légion d'Honneur. When Lanvin died in 1946, aptly her daughter, who had been the catalyst for her mother's career, took over the house.

Opposite This drawing shows Lanvin appealing to two generations with both understated femininity and girlish charm. 1920.

Princesse blanche
Laurin

Combining fluidity and flattery, this
floor-length evening dress from 1932
puts emphasis on defined back detail
and full, softly gathered sleeves.

ON T'ATTEND!

Robe d'organdi et manteau d'enfant, de Jeanne Lanvin

Top Taking a quintessentially French colour palette, Lanvin combines it with pale flowers, fitted bodice and full skirt. 1920.

Above The simplistic structure of this evening dress is infused with sophistication, gathered at the neck and waist, and draped over the shoulder. 1930.

Jeanne Lanvin

1860

1867 — Born in Paris, France

1870

1880 — Trains as dressmaker at House of Talbot and undertakes an apprenticeship at milliner Madame Félix

1889 — Begins hatmaking business in rue Boissy d'Anglais, Paris, before opening on rue du Faubourg Saint-Honoré

1900

1909 — Joins the Syndicat de la Couture

Introduces the 'Robe de Style' bouffant skirted dress

1919 — Establishes interiors business, collaborating with celebrated designer Armand-Albert Rateau

1920 — Awarded Chevalier de la Légion d'Honneur; Menswear introduced into the Lanvin range

1926 — Creates Lanvin Perfumes and launches 'Arpège'

1927

1930

Shows her designs at the Golden Gate International Exposition in San Francisco

1939 — Elected to the governing committee of the Chambre Syndicale de la Couture

1940

Dies in Paris; her daughter Marie-Blanche de Polignac takes over management of the house

1946

1950

'Faithfully antique,
but markedly original.'

Mariano Fortuny

1871–1949

SPAIN

The multitalented Mariano Fortuny became famous for his luminous pleated silk, but he was also a chemist, an artist, an accomplished designer of theatrical sets and an inventor of lighting constellations. Fortuny's Delphos gown, on the surface sublime in its simplicity, was in fact a technical masterpiece. Merging perpendicular folds with Classical form, it became a template for sartorial ingenuity. It also had social implications. Embodying as it did the fundamental beliefs of the Rational and Aesthetic dress movements, the Delphos gown was a symbol of female empowerment. Flowing easily over the body, it celebrated freedom. Fortuny's fashion statement was the polar opposite of the restrictive corsetry of that time.

With artist parents who had their own collection of exquisite antique fabrics, Fortuny was surrounded by aesthetic inspiration as a child. After his father's death, his mother relocated the family from Spain to Paris, where Fortuny began his artistic instruction with Orientalist Jean-Joseph Benjamin-Constant, and in 1889 they moved again to Venice. From an early age, Fortuny enjoyed concocting an experimental colour palette and working out ways of reinventing fabric.

Early in his career, his interests were predominantly theatrical. Fascinated by the thespian world and operatic environments, in 1892 Fortuny travelled to Bayreuth, Germany, to see Wagner's famous theatre. He collaborated with the composer, primarily as a set designer, but also as a lighting technician, patenting a new lamp in 1901 and predicting that 'theatrical scenery will be able to transform itself in tune with music'. Travelling through Europe, Fortuny met his muse and wife-to-be, Henriette Negrin, while in Paris. Returning to

Venice, and with his interest in fashion reinvigorated, in 1906 Fortuny created the Knossos scarf, which was a length of pleated fabric, designed primarily for the theatre. This classic accessory was to be in production for almost a quarter of a century. Fortuny viewed his Delphos dress as an invention rather than a fashion statement, and in 1907 patented not only the design but also the textile-pleating technique.

He opened a boutique in Paris in 1909, which was followed two years later by an exhibition at the Louvre. In 1918 he married Negrin, and a year afterwards opened a factory in the grounds of the former convent on the Venetian island of Giudecca. In 1920 he opened a new shop in Paris, next door to a boutique owned by Paul Poiret (p. 33).

Fortuny was famously secretive, and his methods of fabric manipulation and production were closely guarded. His colour palette was exquisite. 'No other dyer in the world seems to get the marvellous… sea-greens, the rusty autumn-reds, and all the others,' said *Vogue*. The great French novelist Marcel Proust and the American dancer Isadora Duncan were both fans of Fortuny's art. At heart he was a classicist, creating a handful of key silhouettes, which are still synonymous with the Fortuny identity.

Opposite Revolutionary, unrestrictive, and designed to glide over the body, this Fortuny dress has all the hallmarks of classical Greek drapery.

Hand-dyed dress featuring
perpendicular tubular pleating, a
scooped neckline and waist belt
decoration.

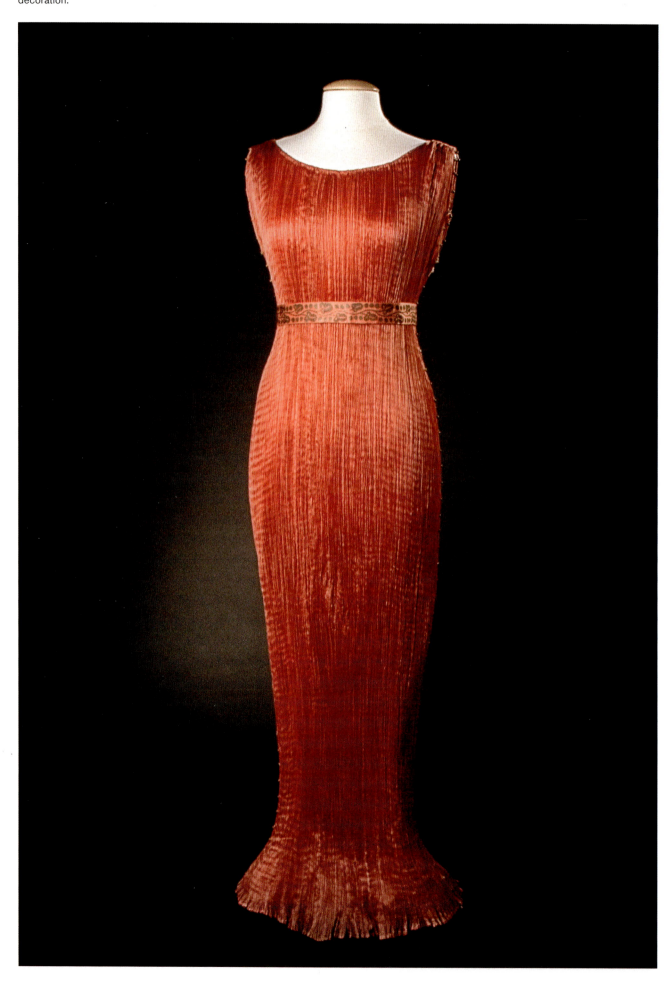

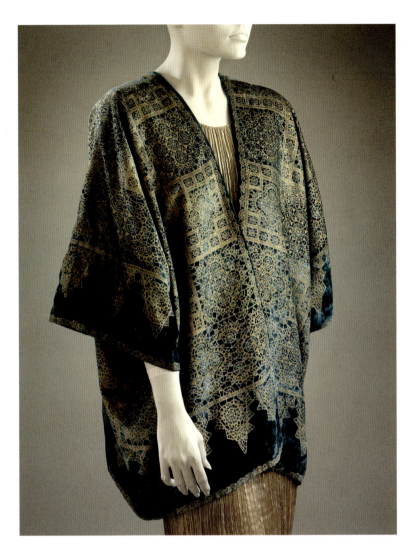

Above Tubular, pleated silk evening dress and square-cut jacket in gold stamped silk velvet, c. 1927.

Below The simple Fortuny accessory: a deep blue, velvet tie-belt with intricate golden overprint.

Mariano Fortuny

1871 Born in Granada, Spain

1880

1889 Studies art at the Accademia in Venice

Discovers Wagner and begins designing for the theatre

1892 Awarded gold medal for his painting *The Flower Girls* at the Munich International Festival of Art

1897 Acquires freehold of Palazzo Orfei, later known as Palazzo Fortuny, Venice

1900

1905 Opens the first Fortuny boutique, located in the Palazzo

1909 Fabbrica Fortuny is founded, equipped with machinery made to Fortuny's specifications

1919

1930

1940

Dies at Palazzo Orfei, Venice, Italy

1949

1960

'I have never insisted on ornaments. I use them on the sole condition that they complement the construction of the dress.'

Madeleine Vionnet

1876–1975

FRANCE

Eliminating everything except the finest fabric and exquisite cut, Madeleine Vionnet dispensed with the standard elements of accentuation and instead celebrated the female form. 'I have proved,' she declared, 'that material falling freely on an uncorseted body was the most harmonious of spectacles.' Inspired by ancient Greek drapery and modern dance, Vionnet believed in fluidity and freedom of movement. Her designs – uncomplicated on the surface, but a result of genius geometry in reality – were to form a landmark in fashion history. Vionnet's trademark – the bias cut – was her basis for these designs. Working three-dimensionally using a miniature mannequin with articulated limbs, Vionnet draped, pinned, sculpted and rearranged crepe and satin to achieve the desired effect. 'For me, the idea of a dress is mental,' she said. 'I conceive it and create it by dreaming. And finally, after searching, I end up holding it in my hands.'

At 17, Vionnet joined the House of Vincent in Paris, where within two years she had become the head seamstress. Employed by Kate Reily in London, and then by Callot Soeurs and Jacques Doucet in Paris, Vionnet eventually opened her own salon in 1912 in Paris. After the war the house reopened with a new financial structure and a logo designed by the Florentine Futurist artist Ernesto Michahelles, known as Thayaht. His drawing of a woman wearing an understated dress standing on a Classical column encased in a circle was the beginning of a collaboration that would include his input on design, colour palette and motifs.

The Vionnet atelier was, in common with Vionnet's approach to making clothes, precise, inventive and incredibly organized. She provided employees with dental and medical care, childcare facilities, a dining room and 21 workshops. In 1925, she launched her first fragrances, their single letter titles A, B, C and D echoing her unpretentious, modern approach to fashion. By 1932, Vionnet had a total of 21 ateliers, but seven years later she planned to retire. She refused to sell her name, and the house was liquidated in 1945. In 1952 she donated the vast majority of her archive to the newly formed Union Française des Arts du Costume. This included 120 dresses from 1921 to 1939, 75 copyright albums and 750 toiles, in addition to account records, table linen, original drawings and part of her personal library. When Vionnet died at the age of 98, ardent admirer Diana Vreeland paid tribute. 'She was the quintessence of elegance,' said Vreeland to the *New York Times*. 'There is no one to compare her with.'

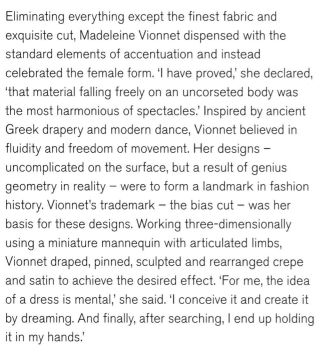

Opposite Arranging fabric in a geometric formation which fell beautifully across the body was the key to Vionnet's genius. 1934.

The potent combination of purity,
exacting proportion and technical
prowess is present in this 1931 gown,
worn by house model Sonia.

Above Two takes on bias cutting: the relative austerity of the wrap paired with the suggestiveness of a revealing evening dress. 1932.

Left The deceptive simplicity of the brand. Underlined by Grecian references, this design by Thayaht was used on headed paper and invitation cards. 1919.

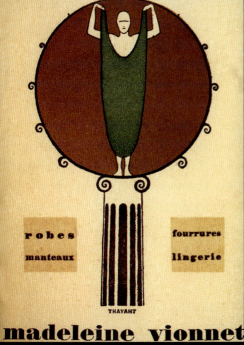

robes   fourrures
manteaux   lingerie

THAYAHT

madeleine vionnet

1876 Born in Loiret, France

1880

1890

1900

1907 Joins designer Jacques Doucet

1912 Founds her own house, Vionnet

1914 The house is closed due to the onset of World War I

1920

1923 House re-established as the 'Temple of Fashion'

1924 First Vionnet garments bearing the 'MV' monogram produced

1929 Awarded the Chevalier de la Légion d'Honneur

Vionnet's genius captured by Vogue photographer George Hoyningen-Huene

1931 Launches 'Temptation' perfume, powder and lipstick

1934

1939 At the outbreak of World War II, Vionnet closes her house

1948 Jacques Fath includes tribute to Vionnet in his 'Hollywood 25 Ball'

1950

1952 Donates her archive to the Union Française des Arts du Costume

1960

City of Paris presents Vionnet with gold medal in recognition of her contribution to fashion

1971

1975 Dies in Paris, France

'I freed the bust,
but shackled the legs.'

Paul Poiret

1879–1944

FRANCE

The pioneering couturier Paul Poiret was a breath of fresh air at the beginning of the twentieth century. During his spectacular career he banished the corset, shackled the legs and introduced a series of revolutionary proportions including harem pants, lampshade tunics and hobble skirts. A brilliant self-publicist, Poiret entered the world of haute couture with the intention of questioning contemporary fashion. 'Am I mad when I try to put art into my dresses, or when I say that couture is an art?' he wondered.

As a teenager, Poiret took his sketches to the most prominent couture houses and Madeleine Chéruit became his first patron, purchasing 12 of his designs. In 1898, by then working for Jacques Doucet, he created a red wool cloak lined in grey crepe de Chine that became a bestseller. However, it was a black tulle and taffeta cloak designed for actress Gabrielle Réjane in a production entitled *Zaza* that would make his name. 'When they saw it appear, the audience foresaw the end of the play… Thenceforth, I was established chez Doucet and in all of Paris,' he recalled. When Poiret left Doucet in 1900 he was already head of the tailoring department; moving to the House of Worth, he was employed specifically to design simple practical garments to counterpoint the extravagant signature pieces.

With the knowledge gleaned from his time at Doucet and Worth, Poiret founded his own house in 1903. He married Denise Boulet, who would become both his muse and his artistic director. Poiret's plans were ambitious – he attempted to banish uniformity and eliminate corsetry. He began to liberate the body by eliminating first the petticoat, then the corset, and showed a preference for uncomplicated classical lines – Greek drapery, the Japanese kimono. Following the success of his costumes for the Ballets Russes' production of *Scheherazade* in 1910, Poiret embraced Orientalism. He staged an extravagant fancy-dress party at his home in Paris that he called 'The Thousand And Second Night', with his wife dressed in silk harem pants, which would inspire his new silhouette.

By 1913, Poiret's reputation had reached America. He toured department stores and delivered a series of lectures. The *New York Times* was definitive in its praise, running the headline 'Poiret, Creator of Fashion Is Here'. When Poiret enlisted into the army as a military tailor at the outbreak of World War I, his house was forced to close.

The relaunch of the House of Poiret after the war was the beginning of its decline. Now, with Chanel (p. 41) as the new name in Paris, Poiret's star was on the descendant. His legendary status was secured, but he died destitute in 1944.

Opposite Sorbet silk evening dress with contrasting peplum and side panel, and hooped hemline, all embroidered with flowers.

Below The perfectly proportioned empire line, draped from the bodice and accessorized with a feathered cloche, from the 1920s.

Opposite Celebrating the abolition of corsetry, Poiret deployed Grecian pleating to symbolize the new freedom in dress and enable ease of movement. 1908

Below right Sumptuous ankle-length devore velvet kimono coat with contrasting sleeves and border. 1922.

Paul Poiret

1879 — Born in Paris, France

1890

1898 — Hired by Jacques Doucet
Joins the House of Worth

1901 — Establishes his own house

1903 — Marries his muse, Denise Boulet

1905 — His album of fashion designs, Les Robes de
Paul Poiret, is published

1908 — Becomes first French couturier to launch a
signature scent – 'Parfums de Rosine'

1911 — Serves as military tailor in the Army

1914 — Business is on the brink of bankruptcy

1919 — His house is closed

1929 — His book on design, On Dressing This Age, is
1930 — followed by his autobiography, My First Fifty Years

1940

1944 — Dies in Paris, France

1950

1960

1970

'Quality is remembered long
after price is forgotten.'

Guccio Gucci

1881–1953

ITALY

The Gucci empire, whose iconic identity pivots on four key symbols, was a product of the founder's acute sense of observation. The interlocking double G, the bamboo handle, the horse bit and the green-and-red web stripe are the hallmarks of a company that started as a modest Florentine saddlery shop and went on to become one of the most recognizable and desirable labels in the world. For almost a century, exclusivity, craftsmanship, longevity and luxury have been at the core of the Gucci brand.

It was while working as a bellboy at the Savoy Hotel in London that Gucci saw his future. The international clientele – aristocratic, rich, elegant and well-travelled – were always accompanied by a cache of sophisticated accessories. On witnessing at first hand these impeccable luggage collections, he found his market.

Born in 1881, the son of an impoverished milliner, Guccio Gucci had left Florence as a teenager to find his fortune in London. His aim on returning to Italy was to blend the inherent taste of the English aristocracy with the instinctive skills of Italian craftsmen. After leaving leather-crafts company Franzi, in 1921 Gucci opened his own store in Florence. His early customers were horse-riding nobility. Their demand for riding accessories inspired the development of the horse-bit insignia – the most enduring Gucci symbol. In 1935 trade restrictions meant Gucci had to extend his range: shoes, belts and wallets were added. A second store was opened in Rome in 1938 on the exclusive Via Condotti.

During the 1940s, with a shortage of supplies, Gucci began to experiment with alternative materials such as jute, linen, hemp and bamboo. The web stripe was taken from a traditional saddle girth. The first bamboo-handled bag, codenamed '0633', was introduced in 1947. Subtler symbols – for example a spotted pigskin from a Scottish tanner – were added to the Gucci design portfolio. In 1951 Gucci opened a store in Milan and, two years later, one in New York.

After the death of Guccio Gucci in 1953, his sons Aldo, Vasco, Ugo and Rodolfo took over the business. Led by Aldo Gucci, the brand went from strength to strength. Inroads were made into the wealthy American market, with the Gucci insignia heralded by the *New York Times* as 'a status symbol recognized around the world'. Having built on its luxurious accessories as a foundation, the Gucci brand now included clothing, and was by the early 1970s firmly fixed in the public consciousness as synonymous with the jet set. The first signature Gucci scent was launched in 1975.

The arrival of Tom Ford (p. 277) in 1994 was instrumental in reconstructing Gucci's identity. Under Ford's direction the company went from the brink of bankruptcy to a $4.3 billion dollar concern. 'I realized that this very traditional house was actually very hip and very cutting-edge in its heyday,' Ford told *Vogue*. 'Why couldn't it be hip and cutting-edge now?'

Opposite Tom Ford makes Gucci hip again with an unbuttoned plunging satin shirt, low-cut velvet trousers, and handbag slung from the shoulders on the Autumn/Winter 1995 catwalk.

Top The height of sophistication: sitting in the doorway of a 1958 Packard Hawk with a travel handbag by Gucci.

Above Slip-on Gucci shoe, c. 1968, with contrasting colour leather and side snaffle detail.

Opposite Veruschka in a top-to-toe Gucci ensemble: hat, shirt, two belts with brass buckles, and print cotton trousers. 1970.

Guccio Gucci

1881 Born in Florence, Italy

1890

1901 After working as a bellboy at the Savoy in London, Gucci returns to Italy to become a luggage maker

1910

1921 Opens his own store in Via della Vigna Nuova, Florence, after working for leather goods company Franzi

1930

1933 Double 'G' Gucci logo designed by Guccio's son, Aldo

1938 Second store opens in Rome

1940

1947 Invention and introduction of first bamboo-handled bag

1951 First store in Milan opens on Via Montenapoleone

1953 Dies in Florence, two weeks after launch of New York boutique

1960

1970

'Luxury is a relaxation of the soul.'

Gabrielle Chanel

1883–1971

FRANCE

A pioneering classicist with a revolutionary attitude, Gabrielle 'Coco' Chanel was a matriarch of modernity. Responsible for introducing a series of firsts into the fashion arena, Chanel followed her instinct, most notably advocating suntans at a time when pale was considered chic. She defiantly used jersey – formerly only deployed in underwear – as outerwear. She promoted androgynous dressing in an era of femininity. She created the ultimate woman's suit, which has lost none of its desirability despite spanning two centuries.

Chanel's life was an extraordinary rags-to-riches tale in which she made the quantum leap from a French poorhouse to the Paris Ritz, mixing with the higher echelons of aristocratic society. Pertinently, she was to observe: 'Some people think luxury is the opposite of poverty. It is not. It is the opposite of vulgarity.'

Financed by her wealthy businessman boyfriend, Arthur 'Boy' Capel, Chanel initially became a milliner, opening a shop near the Ritz. She progressed to sportswear in Deauville in 1913 and couture in Biarritz, opening her couture salon in Paris in 1918. Chanel's iconic perfume, Chanel N°5, was formulated in 1921. With a genius for publicity that matched her aptitude for creating irresistible clothes, such was Chanel's popularity on both sides of the Channel that she opened her first London house in 1927. Her definitive signature – a mix of restrained opulence, understatement, extravagance and elegance – centred on a handful of core statements: the little black dress; the collarless tweed suit; the simple shift dress; the crisp white shirt. Each outfit was worn with strong accessories such as rows of pearls, a camellia, or a quilted leather bag suspended from gold chains. The Chanel signature was one of careful editing, never overdoing. Above all, it was ageless. 'I don't like to hear about the Chanel fashion,' she said, 'Chanel is above all a style. Fashion becomes unfashionable. Style never.' Summoned to Hollywood in 1931, Chanel travelled to make costumes for, among others, Gloria Swanson.

When war broke out in 1939 Chanel closed her salon on the rue Cambon and went into retirement. At the age of 71, in 1954, she made a triumphant comeback. In an interview with *Vogue* she said, 'I am no longer interested in dressing a few hundred women, private clients. I shall dress thousands of women. But a widely repeated fashion seen everywhere must start from luxury. At the top of the pinnacle must be luxe.'

The 1960s saw a Chanel renaissance, with a host of celebrities – Elizabeth Taylor, Grace Kelly and Jeanne Moreau – wearing her classic suit. Chanel was immortalized on Broadway in a musical called *Coco*, starring Katharine Hepburn, with costumes by Cecil Beaton. It was not until 1978, after Chanel's death, that the label made the transition from couture to ready-to-wear.

Opposite A modern take on the traditional Chanel jacket, with fitted body and fluted sleeves, paired with faded denim jeans. Photographed by Karl Lagerfeld.

Below Defying the extreme abbreviation of 1960s mainstream fashion, the tweed suit consisting of collarless jacket and slimline skirt retains its popularity. 1958.

Opposite Tailored to perfection, the double breasted wool suit features signature gilt buttons with strategically placed chains. Lagerfeld for Chanel, 1983.

Gabrielle Chanel

Born in Saumur, France

Meets Arthur 'Boy' Capel who finances her first shop

Opens first boutique in Deauville, Normandy; causes a sensation when she uses jersey for outerwear

Opens couture salon in Biarritz

Formulates and launches her first fragrance, Chanel Nº5, with celebrated perfumer Ernest Beaux

Introduces the Little Black Dress, hailed by American Vogue as 'the frock that all the world will wear'

Launches fine jewellery collection in her private salon in Paris

1880 **1883** 1890 1900 **1908** 1910 **1913 1915** 19 **1921** **1926** 1930 **1932**

When war is announced, the couture
house closes

'71-year-old Chanel makes her return
to haute couture

Creates the two-tone sling shoe

N°19 perfume launched
Dies in her apartment at the Ritz Hotel, Paris

1939 '40   1950   1954 1957 1960   1970 '71   1980   1990

'I like to see women look slightly exotic.'

Elsa Schiaparelli

1890–1973

ITALY

The arch-rival of Chanel (p. 41), Surrealist experimentalist Elsa Schiaparelli was a nonconformist whose imagination knew no bounds. 'She was bigger than life in the way she saw things and expressed things,' recalled her granddaughter, model Marisa Berenson. 'She was full of ideas. She had tremendous imagination and fantasy about everything, including her own life.' Unafraid to turn a shoe into a hat or acrobats into buttons, or to sprinkle metallic insects on to a clear plastic collar, Schiaparelli was heavily influenced by the artistic clique she was part of, which included Man Ray, Christian Bérard, Salvador Dalí and Jean Cocteau. Academically untrained, but encouraged by Paul Poiret (p. 33), Schiaparelli transformed her natural love of knitwear into a viable collection with trompe-l'oeil images and double-layered stitching. 'She goes everywhere, knows everybody, follows all the artistic activities of painting, sculpture, music and the theatre,' wrote *Vogue* in 1931.

Born in Rome in 1890, Schiaparelli made her first trip to Paris in 1913 and moved to New York in 1916. On divorcing her husband in 1921, Schiaparelli worked as a translator and seamstress to make ends meet. A gregarious woman who was socially at ease, by 1922 she had met Marcel Duchamp, Man Ray, Poiret and Dadaist painter Francis Picabia. In the same year she returned to Paris, opening her first atelier on the rue de Seine designing knitwear and sportswear. Five years later she relocated to the rue de la Paix, producing a bestselling trompe-l'oeil sweater that incorporated a huge bow. She was heralded by the press as 'one of the rare creative talents', as her reputation continued to gain momentum.

Throughout the 1930s she continued to break boundaries. The House of Schiaparelli became notable for its extraordinary interior, with black wooden furniture and patent leather curtains. The introduction of Parfums Schiaparelli included a trio called Salut (for evening), Souci (for town) and Schiap (for sports). Schiaparelli incorporated zips into a series of separates, popularizing the fastener in the context of high fashion. She continued her Surrealist collaborations, first with Dalí, designing a suit where the pockets resembled a chest of drawers, and later designing a coat with Jean Cocteau. Her signature colour, 'shocking pink', was introduced in 1937.

Schiaparelli's artistry and ability to interpret Surrealism in fashion were matched by her accomplishment as a businesswoman. She diversified into lingerie, sunglasses and handbags, each item infused with her avant-garde edge. Of her famous grandmother, Marisa Berenson said: 'Her designs have come full circle. I would want to wear them now. You can't even believe that they were made in that period of time, they are still so incredibly modern.'

Opposite Illustrated by René Bouët-Willaumez, these three women wearing Schiaparelli daywear originallly appeared in the October 15, 1932 issue of *Vogue*.

Opposite Surrealism taken to its extreme in a felt shoe hat and tailored suit in Ducharne's satin decorated with glistening embroidered red lips from the Winter 1937/8 collection.

Right Originally vivid blue jersey (now faded to lavender), this coat is based on a Cocteau drawing of two faces in profile, translated into an embroidered urn topped with roses by Lesage. 1937.

Below Inspired by Salvador Dalí's surreal lobster telephone, this painted silk muslin dress is from the collection of the Duchess of Windsor. 1937.

Elsa Schiaparelli

1880

1890 Born in Rome, Italy

1900

1904 Writes a book of poems entitled *Arethusa* which scandalizes her family

1910

1916 Moves to New York, meeting artists Marcel Duchamp and Dadaist painter Francis Picabia

1920 Moves to Paris and meets Paul Poiret

1922 Designs for Maison Lambal

1925 Produces her famous Trompe l'Oeil bow sweater which is featured in American *Vogue*

1927 Opens a boutique selling ready-to-wear, followed by a London salon

1930

1932 Moves into her Paris headquarters at 21 place Vendôme; popularizes the zip fastener

1935 Receives Neiman Marcus Fashion Award and begins a US lecture tour entitled Clothes and the Woman'

1940 Hubert de Givenchy joins to work as head of her boutique

1947 Introduces menswear, separates and folding sunglasses

1950

1953
1954 Publishes her autobiography *Shocking Life* and retires

1960

1970 Dies in Paris, France

1973

'Couture is the exquisite grammar and syntax of the language of fashion.'

Mainbocher

1890–1976

UNITED STATES

A former editor of French *Vogue* who was credited with 'knowing more about the American woman's figure than any living human', Chicago-born Mainbocher built his reputation on understated, unpretentious elegance. He was a master of the subtle silhouette and chic detail. His most famous and enduring client was Wallis Simpson: creating the blue wedding dress and trousseau for her marriage to the Duke of Windsor, Mainbocher later named the colour 'Wallis blue'. The antithesis of ostentation, Mainbocher's style was one that suggested luxury and whispered self-assurance. 'I'm not designing for obsolescence,' he declared. 'What I'm really about, what I really stand for, is simplicity – reassuring clothes.'

Known professionally as Mainbocher (his full name was Main Rousseau Bocher), the designer who came to symbolize affluent post-war America was an illustrator and magazine editor before he decided to change direction and focus on fashion design. Having worked at both *Harper's Bazaar* as its Paris-based illustrator and French *Vogue* as editor, Mainbocher had a critical eye and an educated overview of international style. His favourite couturier was Madeleine Vionnet (p. 29). Mainbocher resigned from his editorship at *Vogue* in 1929 to become a fashion designer.

On opening his Parisian *maison de couture* at 12 Avenue George V in 1929, his reputation was such that he immediately began to receive orders and became the first American to become a member of the Chambre Syndicale de la Haute Couture. *Vogue* was charting his meteoric rise. 'Here is a new star in the firmament of the Paris couture,' said the magazine in 1932. 'This is only his second year as a dressmaker, yet his name is made.' Mainbocher continued to quietly innovate, introducing the sheath dress ('four seams and a little band around the neck') and creating the 'Mainbocher corset', which was

immortalized by Horst P. Horst in one of his most famous photographs (opposite).

In 1940, after the start of World War II, Mainbocher relocated to New York, with Christian Dior (p. 73) supporting him, saying: 'We are all equals, but Mainbocher is really in advance of us all, because he does it in America.' Mainbocher's clients were the elite of Manhattan society: Diana Vreeland, C. Z. Guest and Babe Paley, to name a few. His prices were among the highest in the world and he justified the monetary outlay with the longevity of his products: 'Our collections glide into one another,' he said.

During the 1960s, Mainbocher was still considered relevant, his collections photographed by Horst and Irving Penn. In 1971 he closed his New York salon after 40 years in the business, donating his collection of drawings to the New York Metropolitan Museum. Mainbocher remained the favourite designer of eccentric fashion editor Isabella Blow, who related to a comment made by writer Anita Loos in 1961: 'I've had my best times when trailing a Mainbocher evening gown across a sawdust floor. I've always loved high style in low company.'

Opposite A portrait of beauty, modesty, balance and sensuality, this corset was famously photographed by Horst in the studios of Paris *Vogue*, 1939.

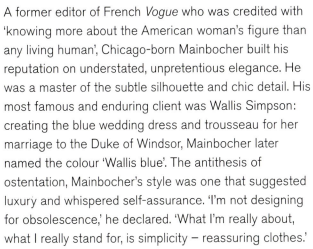

Wallis Simpson's 1937 wedding suit consisted of a bias-cut dress and a jacket with draped bodice detail. A matching slip in Wallis Blue was also provided.

Mainbocher

1890 Born Main Rousseau Bocher in Chicago, USA

19 00

1908 Studies at the University of Chicago

Enrols at Königlich Kunstgewerbemuseum Munich

1911 Becomes an illustrator for *Harper's Bazaar*

1917 Appointed Editor of French *Vogue*

1920

1922 Fuses his first and last name and establishes his own couture house at 12 Avenue George V in Paris

1929 Wallis Simpson marries the Duke of Windsor in a Mainbocher dress

1937 Horst P. Horst famously photographs Mainbocher's 'waist cinch' corset

1939 Commissioned to design uniforms for Girl Scouts and the US Women's Marine Corps

1948

195 0

1961 Moves business to 609 Fifth Avenue, New York

1971 At the age of 81, closes his salon and donates his archive to the Metropolitan Museum of Art, New York

1976 Dies in Munich, Germany

1980

Above Socialite, fashion icon and high-profile client C. Z. Guest was attracted to unfussy, clean tailoring that also featured discreet detail.

Above right Bold print in a subtle colourway, masterfully cut to complement the proportion and pattern of the fabric.

'It's the fabric that decides.'

Cristóbal Balenciaga

1895–1972

SPAIN

Considered fashion's equivalent of Michelangelo, Cristóbal Balenciaga elevated couture to a fine art. Exquisite examples of his life's work are dotted around the world's galleries, hailed as the most enduring exponents of perfection. Revered by Chanel (p. 41) and Dior (p. 73), Balenciaga set the standard for his craft. He became a benchmark by which every other designer measured themselves.

A fervent believer in subtraction rather than detraction, Balenciaga always put sophistication before any kind of sensation. He said it succinctly: 'Elegance is elimination.' Unlike Dior, Balenciaga did not dominate the headlines or become infamous for introducing a new silhouette. His genius lay in unparalleled technique paired with an incredible eye for proportion. He was a quiet revolutionary, whose style centred on a divine chemical reaction, an affinity with fabric and form.

A former altar boy, Balenciaga was born in a fishing village in the Basque town of Getaria; his mother was a seamstress, his father a ferryboat captain. As an adolescent, he secured his first client – the wealthy Marquesa de Casa Torres – who supported him financially, enabling him to leave grammar school and study tailoring in Madrid.

Balenciaga's first salon opened in San Sebastián but closed, bankrupt, during the Spanish Civil War. It reopened in August 1937 in Paris, where it was Balenciaga's refined line that captured the imagination of the audience and changed the history of Paris couture forever. Fashion editor Diana Vreeland later commented: 'No one has ever entered Paris and completely taken over French dressmaking as this strong Spaniard did with his stark, scrupulous shapes.'

Balenciaga's signature was a synergy of precision and proportion, with the two elements being constantly readdressed. Many of his creations were rooted in the visual landscape of his Spanish childhood – recurring themes included bullfighters with their matador jackets and flamenco dancers with their voluminous skirts.

Cultivating an aura of unattainability, Balenciaga was in a position to cherry-pick his clients, dressing only those who followed his fashion philosophy. In 1953, Hubert de Givenchy (p. 117) became Balenciaga's protégé, later giving a glimpse into his notoriously private mentor's life by saying: 'He had the most beautiful breakfast tray I'd ever seen.' Emanuel Ungaro (p. 145) and André Courrèges (p. 113) followed. When Courrèges left to set up his own house in 1961, it was Balenciaga who offered a loan to enable his dream to come to fruition.

Out of kilter with the Swinging Sixties, as the decade drew to an end Balenciaga departed the couture scene. It was May 1968. He had worked in Paris for 30 years. While students rioted in the streets, Balenciaga closed the door on an era, saying there was no one left to dress. Vreeland summed up his legacy: 'In a Balenciaga you were the only woman in the room – no other woman existed.'

Opposite A balance of drapery, angular neckline cutting, and a curvaceous silhouette are present in this perfect 1952 suit.

With a gentle nod to his Spanish roots,
Balenciaga adds silk taffeta flounces,
ruched in various places, that contrast
with the purple velvet evening coat.
1951.

Top A dramatic wingspan hat and elegant triple row of pearls accentuate the outstanding tailoring technique of this longer-line 1948 suit.

Above Strapless, silk satin evening dress with crossover jacket in sheer silk faille, embroidered with fringed glass beads, c. 1955.

1890

1895 — Born in Getaria, Spain

1900

1910

1919 — Opens his first salon in San Sebastián, Spain

1930

1936 — Exiled to Paris during Spanish Civil War; First featured in *Vogue*

1940

1945 — Balenciaga takes part in the 'Théâtre de la Mode'

1950

1953 — Meets Hubert de Givenchy

1960

1968 — Air France commissions Balenciaga to design new uniform for 6,000 employees; closes house

1970

1972 — Dies of a heart attack while heading back to Valencia, Spain

1980

'New fashion begins in
the mind of the designer.'

Salvatore Ferragamo

1898–1960

ITALY

Known historically as the 'shoemaker to the stars', Salvatore Ferragamo shod the gamut of Hollywood royalty during his long and distinguished career. Bette Davis, Vivien Leigh, Rita Hayworth, Katharine Hepburn and Marlene Dietrich were just some of the stars who wore Ferragamo. More than a designer, he was an inventor, redrawing the shape of the heel and redefining the proportion of the foot. His most marked revolution was using previously unconsidered materials in a new way. A craftsman, Ferragamo introduced new materials and methods, had more than 20,000 models in his shoe library and held over 350 patents. Two of the most revolutionary were the cork wedge and gloved arch.

In 1914 Ferragamo emigrated from his native town of Bonito, southern Italy, to join his brother in a Boston shoe factory before moving to California. By then an accomplished shoemaker, he undertook repairs and made custom-designed shoes for many silent-movie stars. These were pleasing to the eye but relatively uncomfortable to wear, and Ferragamo studied anatomy to understand the natural movement and mechanics of the human foot.

Ferragamo returned to Italy in 1927, opening a workshop in Florence, with an enviable international client list ranging from Eva Perón to Marilyn Monroe. However, as America became caught in the throes of the Great Depression and orders diminished, Ferragamo faced financial difficulties, filing for bankruptcy in 1933. Economic restrictions and scarcity of materials sparked a brainwave: he began experimenting with wine corks and

created the wedge heel. Ferragamo explained: 'There is no end to the materials a shoemaker may use to decorate his creations so that every woman may be shod like a princess, and a princess like a fairy queen.' *Vogue* called him 'the wonderful little shoemaker of Florence'.

By 1938, business was booming again and a decade later he had opened a boutique on Park Avenue, New York, and had a workforce of approximately 700 artisans producing 350 pairs of handmade shoes per day. Ferragamo was invited to collaborate with Parisian couturiers Christian Dior (p. 73) and Elsa Schiaparelli (p. 45). His revolutionary designs continued with the metal-cage heel, but his *pièce de résistance* was the flat ballerina pump he created for Audrey Hepburn in *Sabrina* (1954). Marilyn Monroe wore his open-toed slingbacks in *The Seven Year Itch* (1955). In his autobiography he relayed anecdotes about some of his most famous clients; Marlene Dietrich, he said, 'wears the shoes once or twice, enjoys their beauty to the full, then casts them aside'.

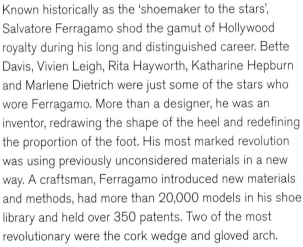

Opposite Focusing on his gloved suede arch, these precisely proportioned shoes feature a circular heel and high-rise insert front.

Above Row upon row of wooden shoe lasts – ranging from Greta Garbo to Gloria Swanson – hung in the studio. A virtual who's who of Hollywood.

Below A trio of cork wedges, invented as a direct consequence of the scarcity of materials. Ferragamo also used raffia, cellophane and fish skin.

Salvatore Ferragamo

1890

1898 Born in Bonito, Italy

1900

1907 Makes his first pair of shoes

1910

1912 Apprenticed to Naples shoemaker before returning to Bonito, Italy

1914 Emigrates to America, learning mass production techniques at Boston's Queen Quality Shoes

1920

1923 Moves to Los Angeles and establishes the Hollywood Boot Shop

1927 Returns to Italy and founds the Ferragamo brand

1930

1936 Experiments with cork and wood, introducing the wedge heel

1938 Opens stores in London and Rome

1940

1948 Park Avenue Ferragamo boutique opens

1950

1954 Creates ballerina shoe for Audrey Hepburn in *Sabrina*

1957 Publishes autobiography entitled *Shoemaker of Dreams*

1960 Dies in Florence, Italy

1970

1980

Lucio Venna's colourful, Cubist
advertisement for Ferragamo. 1930.

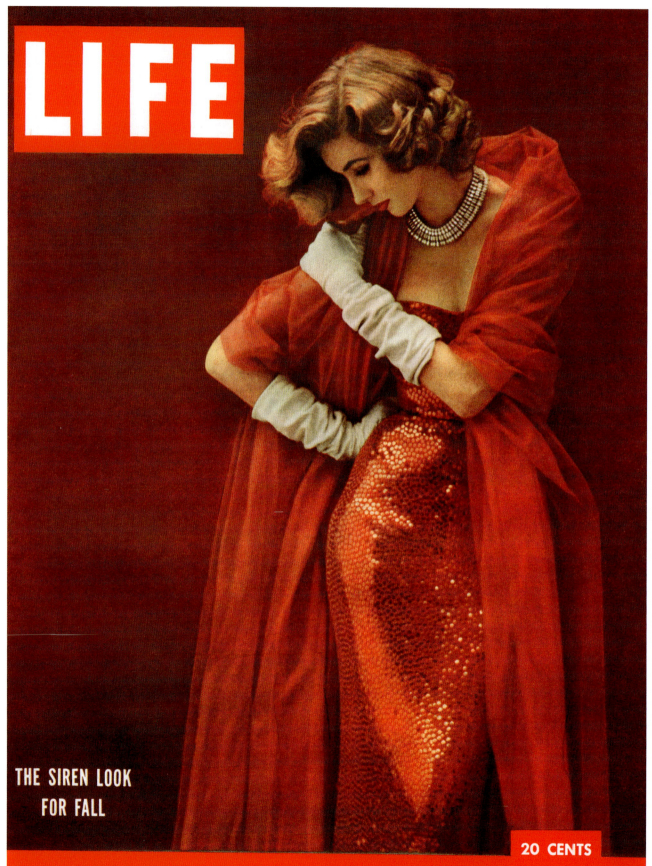

LIFE

THE SIREN LOOK
FOR FALL

20 CENTS

SEPTEMBER 8, 1952

G. U. S. PAT. OFF.

'I don't give a damn about creating. I like to influence fashion, and timing is part of that.'

Norman Norell

1900–1972

UNITED STATES

Known as the 'dean of American fashion', Norman Norell was a designer whose sophisticated eye and matter-of-fact manner won him numerous awards and legions of loyal customers. 'I go with ideas I can stand to look at three months later,' he said, explaining his detached editing process. Not associated with a groundbreaking revolution or a definitive signature silhouette, Norell instead became synonymous with a certain kind of Manhattan elegance and simplicity. It is a style Norell was instrumental in forming. He believed that 'fashion's function is to enhance the beauty of a woman… it changes constantly because women want it to.' His background as a costume designer meant he had a chameleon-like quality, equally comfortable designing a pair of slacks as he was a full-blown ballgown. Whether the garment was essentially casual or conservative, Norell infused an ease and beauty into every seam.

Born Norman David Levinson in Noblesville, Indiana, from an early age he harboured ambitions to be an artist. Straight out of college he joined the New York studio of Paramount Pictures, designing outfits for the major silent-movie stars. He became a costume designer on Broadway specializing in making clothes for performers at the Cotton Club and extravagant confections for the Ziegfeld Follies. In 1928 he was hired by Hattie Carnegie and changed direction, applying his expertise to the mass market. In 1941 he then entered into partnership with Anthony Traina, a wholesale clothing manufacturer.

Here, Norell flourished, and his designs became famous for their immaculate fit and exquisite simplicity. Twice-yearly shows were held as black-tie events to present the new seasons' collections. The recipient of five Coty awards, on his retirement in 1960 he opened his own company under the Norell name.

Adhering to the ethos of 'quality, not quantity', Norell had an innate understanding of Paris couture, which he applied to American ready-to-wear. Considered in the same league as the crème de la crème of Parisian couturiers, Norell is considered one of the original formulators of the New York style, paving the way for Bill Blass, James Galanos and in particular Halston (p. 137). Norell died in October 1972, just as he was to receive the ultimate accolade: a retrospective exhibition of his work at the Metropolitan Museum of New York. Michelle Obama, First Lady of the United States, made fashion history when she wore a vintage Norell dress to a Washington Christmas party in December 2010. It was the first time a first lady had worn vintage to a public event, and testament to the timelessness of Norell's work.

Opposite The coveted cover of *Life* magazine makes a definitive statement on that season's siren look: Norell's ruby sequinned dress and swathe of organza. 1952.

Above Lauren Bacall wears contrasting sugar pink proportions – a generous bias-cut shoulder drape with the narrowest diamanté buckled belt.

Left Effortless glamour encapsulated in a glittering sleeveless floor length evening dress, seamed at the waist. 1953.

Opposite This satin-backed crepe dress in coffee and cream features an abbreviated funnel neck, side split, waist tie, and subtle ruching under the bodice. 1962.

Norman Norell

1890

1900 — Born Norman David Levinson in Noblesville, Indiana, USA

1910

1918 — Attends Parsons School of Design Studies at Pratt Institute, Brooklyn

1920 — Joins the Astoria Studio at Paramount Pictures

1922 — designing costumes for silent movie stars, including Gloria Swanson

1928 — Hired by Hattie Carnegie

1930

1941 — Goes into business with Anthony Traina to form Traina Norell

1943 — Wins Coty American Fashion Critics Award

1950

1956 — Inducted into the Coty Hall of Fame; Parsons award him a medal for Distinguished Achievement

1960 — Opens his own company and launches his own label

1970

1972 — Dies in New York, USA

1980

Norman Hartnell.

'I despise simplicity. It is the negation of all that is beautiful.'

Norman Hartnell

1901–1979

UNITED KINGDOM

Sir Norman Hartnell was the urbane English designer who combined romanticism, theatricality and propriety in equal measure. Discreet and discerning, he not only became famous for being the official dressmaker to the Queen, but also was responsible for dressing two generations of the British royal family. 'My interest in fashion began with a box of crayons,' he wrote in his 1955 autobiography *Silver and Gold*, recalling how he drew pictures of frocks on the front of his mathematics schoolbooks. From this inauspicious beginning, he progressed to being commissioned to create the coronation gown worn by Queen Elizabeth II at Westminster Abbey. This was the scene of Hartnell's finest hour. 'Such splendour I had never seen before and may never see again,' he said.

Hartnell read modern languages at Cambridge, but left a year early without completing his degree. More interested in stage design than studying, he became involved with the Footlights Dramatic Club. 'Is the dress genius of the future now in Cambridge?' asked a reviewer in the London *Evening Standard*. Hartnell decided on a career in fashion and was employed briefly at court outfitters Madame Desiree. On 23 April 1923 – St George's Day – he decided that he would go it alone. With '£300, a box of paints and the enthusiasm of ignorance', Hartnell opened a salon on Bruton Street in London's Mayfair.

Hartnell was already in demand as a society couturier, and his royal association began with an invitation to design the wedding dress for Lady Alice Montagu-Douglas-Scott, whose bridesmaids were to include the young princesses Margaret and Elizabeth – the future Queen Elizabeth II. In May 1937, Hartnell was summoned to Buckingham Palace, the first of many visits. In 1947, when Princess Elizabeth's engagement was announced, Hartnell was given less than three months to complete the wedding dress and train. On the death of her father, Elizabeth became Queen and in October 1952, Hartnell was also asked to design her coronation gown. He produced nine variations, which 'began in almost severe simplicity and proceeded towards elaboration'. Hand-embroidered with 10,000 seed pearls and thousands of white crystal beads, the final version contained symbols of England, Ireland, Scotland and Wales. The Queen's verdict was: 'Glorious.'

Hartnell choreographed the wardrobes of both the Queen and the Queen Mother. For the Queen he constructed a pragmatic, elegant persona, appropriate for a royal who was visible on the world stage; for the Queen Mother a more romantic image, reminiscent of a Winterhalter portrait. After 40 years of designing for royalty, in 1977, Hartnell, who admitted he was 'more than partial to the jolly glitter of sequins', was made a Knight Commander of the Victorian Order.

Opposite The final illustrated design for the coronation dress of Queen Elizabeth II created by Hartnell. The dress featured exquisitely intricate embroidery depicting the floral symbols of the British Isles.

Left The ultimate in English understatement: draped bodice, tapered skirt, loosely cut jacket, elbow-length sleeves and low-slung pearls. 1959.

Above An early fashion illustration, c. 1923, has shades of flapper dressing with fluted organza hemline and flared sleeves.

Opposite Swathes of fur highlight the iridescent glamour of this intricately cut, gold lamé evening dress, gathered at strategically placed points. 1944.

Norman Hartnell

Born in London, England

Studies at Magdalene College, Cambridge

Assists court dressmaker Madame Desiree before opening his studio at Bruton Street, Mayfair

Appointed dressmaker to the Royal Family

One of the founders of the Incorporated Society of London Fashion Designers

Shows collection in South America and Eva Perón becomes a client

Designs Queen Elizabeth II's wedding dress

Creates coronation gown for Queen Elizabeth II

19 | 1901 | 1910 | 19 | '21 '23 | 1930 | 1938 1940 1942 | '46 '47 | 1950 | 1953

'For a dress to survive from one period to the next, it has to be imbued with extreme purity.'

Madame Grès

1903–1993

FRANCE

For more than half a century Madame Grès was unwavering in her creative vision and relentless in her quest for couture perfection. Working under three separate pseudonyms – Alix Barton, Alix Grès and finally Madame Grès – the sculptress formerly known as Germaine Émilie Krebs became synonymous with sublime classicism. Frequently referred to as the sphinx of haute couture, she echoed marble tones in her preferred palette: alabaster, oyster-grey, ivory. 'For me, working fabric or stone is the same thing,' she said.

Grès began studying couture in an atelier and briefly became a milliner before opening La Maison Alix in 1932. A year later she and another couturier, Juliette Barton, combined to create Alix Barton, selling garment prototypes to Europe and America. With a growing reputation as an intellectual, Grès was described in the fashion magazine *L'Officiel* as 'the brainy artist, whose creative skill has forthwith placed Maison Alix Barton in the first flight'. Dissolving the partnership with Barton, at her first Alix presentation, she showed silk jersey for the first time.

In 1942 she created the Grès label, opening the doors to her new salon at 1 rue de la Paix, an address she would keep until her business closed. When German forces occupied Paris during World War II, Grès defied the occupation by displaying a group of evening gowns in the colours of the French tricolour. 'I was doing the opposite of everything I was supposed to do,' she said later. In 1945, after the end of the war, Grès contributed to the international touring exhibition of miniature mannequins entitled 'Théâtre de la Mode'.

Flirting with the idea of making a ready-to-wear collection, in 1951 Grès launched a line of day clothes under the label 'Grès Shop'. She visited New York for the first time in 1956; the *New York Times* commented on 'her artist's hands, swift as humming birds, darting over the material as she shapes it'. Her business was unwavering in its vision throughout the next two decades. In 1980, Madame Grès reluctantly agreed to commercialize her name, creating a ready-to-wear line that included accessories – scarves and later ties – but haute couture remained her abiding passion. 'I have nothing to say and everything to do,' she said. 'All I do is work, work, work. When I'm not sleeping, I'm cutting. That's my life.'

Madame Grès showed her last collection of 21 pieces in 1988, five years before her death. The company was liquidated but her legacy lives on.

Opposite During the 1940s, while fashion focused on utility, Grès continued to develop her fluid draping, precise stitching and floor-sweeping proportions.

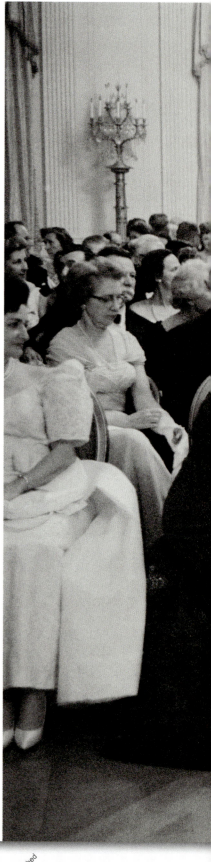

Above Daywear courtesy of Grès contained the signature hallmarks of Grecian pleating but with pared-down detail and shorter hemlines. Drawing by Isola.

Left Dramatic, effective, deceptively simple: an evening ensemble designed to make an unforgettable exit. 1937.

Opposite Jacqueline Kennedy takes a break from tradition, wearing a Grecian dress, draped from the waist and secured at the shoulder at a White House reception for the Nobel prize winners in 1962.

Madame Grès

Born Germaine Émilie Krebs in Paris, France

Establishes her house 'Alix' and designs black, bias-cut cellophane dress, photographed by Hoyningen-Huene and featured in *Vogue*

Marries Russian artist Serge Anatolievitch Czerefkow, who signed his work 'Gres'

Relaunches her design house under the name Grès

Last collection before the liberation of Paris is presented in the red, white and blue of the French flag

1900	**1903**	1910	1920	1930 **1932**	**1937**	1940 **1942** **'44** 1950

Elected President of the Chambre
Syndicale de la Couture Parisienne

First recipient of the Dé D'Or (Golden Thimble
Award); accessories line introduced

Creation of first ready-to-wear collection

Retires after Spring/Summer collection
presentation

Dies in the south of France

1970 · 1972 · 1976 · 1980 · 1988 · 990 · 1993 · 2000 · 2010

'I brought back the neglected art of pleasing.'

Christian Dior

1905–1957

FRANCE

One look – the New Look – was enough to define Christian Dior's legacy and secure his place in fashion history. Sandwiched between the austerity of the war years and the advent of the teenager, Dior's pivotal proportions stunned the public and grabbed the global headlines. He was 41 years old at the time. His audacious, undulating sensation – voluminous skirt, curvaceous seams, cinched waist and pristine line – was unleashed on an unsuspecting world at 10.30 am on 12 February 1947. *Time* magazine retrospectively described the groundbreaking moment in radical terms: 'Never in the history of fashion had a single designer made such a revolution in his first showing.' A decade later, Dior became the first fashion designer to feature on the magazine's cover.

Having studied political science in Paris, Dior served in the French Army before working as an illustrator, art dealer and designer at both Piguet and Lelong. From the outset, he had an uncomplicated vision of his creative output: 'clothes that would give the impression of simplicity would in fact involve elaborate workmanship and would be aimed at a clientele of really elegant women.' Founded in December 1946, and backed by wealthy textile financier Marcel Boussac, the House of Dior presented its first collection in 1947. Originally called 'Corolle' and 'Huit', the collection was re-christened the 'New Look' by the editor-in-chief of *Harper's Bazaar*, Carmel Snow. The polar opposite of wartime make-do-and-mend, the New Look's most marked characteristic was its full skirt, ending below mid-calf and comprising up to 20 metres (65 feet) of fabric. Afterwards, on a tour to the United States, placards from suffragette housewives greeting his arrival

declared 'Down with the New Look', and even 'Burn Monsieur Dior'.

Calling himself a 'shy, shrinking character' and described by *Life* magazine as looking like a 'French undertaker', Dior was rotund and his own clothes larger than life. He was commissioned to dress Marlene Dietrich in *Stage Fright* (1950) and Ava Gardner in *The Little Hut* (1957), while actress Lauren Bacall was a fixture at his shows. Fashion apart, Dior was also an accomplished writer. In the *Little Dictionary of Fashion* (1954) he mused, among other things, on the minutiae of armholes, stating that 'if the sleeve sits badly the whole design is ruined'. He published his autobiography, *Dior by Dior*, in 1957.

The New Look could not be surpassed – in terms of either originality or impact – despite a succession of inventive ideas: the Oblique line in 1950, the Oval and Envol lines in 1951, the Princess and Profile lines in 1952. These were followed by the H line, the A line and the Y line. Each collection garnered a positive reaction but never equalled the authority of the New Look. 'As long as I live, whatever triumphs I win, nothing will ever exceed my feelings at that supreme moment,' said Dior, who died prematurely at the age of 52.

Opposite Layers of silk chiffon softly draping at pivotal points are tied at the waist and paired with elongated gloves, satin shoes and a straw hat. 1956.

Opposite The Y line of 1955–56, personified by an angular waist-level insert which accentuates the figure and gives the illusion of streamlining.

Left The Oblique line of Autumn/Winter 1950–51 echoes the New Look with its cinched waist and full skirt.

Below Dior's revolutionary New Look of 1947 was notable for its wasp waist, sinuous silhouette and extravagant skirt.

Christian Dior

1900

1905 Born in Granville, France

1910

1919 Attends Lycée Gerson, Paris

1930

1935 Takes up fashion drawing – drawings later purchased by Robert Piguet, who also employs him

1940

1946 Opens his own house
1947 Launches the 'New Look'

1950 Establishes licences for accessories, hosiery and lingerie

1957 Publishes autobiography *Dior by Dior*; dies of a heart attack in Italy; Yves Saint Laurent named as his successor

1960

1970

1980

1990

'Each new collection starts with the idea of comfort, need, fun.'

Claire McCardell

1905–1958

UNITED STATES

'Clothes may make the woman, but the woman can also make the clothes. When a dress runs away with a woman, it's a horror,' Claire McCardell told *Time* magazine in 1955. The pragmatic and clear-thinking McCardell was the precursor to Donna Karan. Her groundbreaking philosophy on functionality laid the foundation for the modern all-American wardrobe. 'I've always designed things I needed myself,' she said. 'It just turns out that other people needed them too.'

McCardell's rationale – that every garment must have a reason – was a revolutionary concept in the mid-1950s. Anti-frivolity and opposed to any kind of superfluous detail, McCardell made her name, and her fortune, with her Monastic and Popover dresses, proclaiming that she liked 'buttons that button and sashes that tie'.

Born in Frederick, Maryland, to a banker father and Southern belle mother, McCardell was a tomboy who applied her passion for fitness to her fashion approach. Specializing in illustration at Parsons School of Design (then the New York School of Fine and Applied Arts), in her second year she attended the school's Paris branch. Returning to New York, she became an assistant to Robert Turk. When he closed his business she joined him at Townley Frocks, and after Turk died in 1932, McCardell stepped in to finish the collection. She described her first fashion hit – the Monastic dress – as a 'flowing robe-like design that the wearer shaped to her own waistline with a sash or belt'. Between Townley's closing and reopening, McCardell worked briefly for Hattie Carnegie, but McCardell did not aspire to make faux couture or diluted versions of Parisian fashion and the working relationship was short-lived. Returning to Townley, McCardell focused on mass production. In 1934 she launched interchangeable separates – a new

phenomenon – and with different fabrication, she blurred boundaries, making an evening dress in cotton shirting, for example, instead of silk. She took cloth that was fundamentally workwear – denim, fleece, seersucker, ticking, calico – and reinterpreted it. 'The line is clearly dictated by the character of the fabric, each silhouette depending entirely on its material for shape.' It was McCardell who popularized the ballet slipper as everyday wear and designed a diaper bathing suit.

By 1942, McCardell was becoming a brand. Her denim Popover dress sold a total of 75,000 within a year and in 1945 *Vogue* published a portrait of McCardell in a dress 'made entirely of two huge triangles that tie at the neck, back and front'. An admirer of Madeleine Vionnet (p. 29) and Madame Grès (p. 69), McCardell was the recipient of many honours. In 1990, 32 years after her death, *Life* magazine named her as one of the 100 most important Americans of the twentieth century. 'The typical McCardell girl looked comfortable in her clothes because she was comfortable,' *Vogue* editor Sally Kirkland had observed in the 1940s. 'She always had deep side pockets, even in evening dresses, which encouraged a sort of nonchalant Astaire-like stance.'

Opposite Setting the tone for American-style ready-to-wear, McCardell creates a ruched strapless sundress and asymmetric wrap. 1947.

Opposite A playful sunsuit with side buttoning, constructed from stretch jersey, with a plunging neckline.

Below This functional cotton dress, designed for American manufacturer Townley Frocks in 1942, features wide sleeves, large side pocket and button-through waist.

Above Military detailing re-drawn, re-proportioned and re-invented in this relaxed sportswear outfit of long-line shorts and unbuttoned shirt worn over a jersey polo sweater. 1949.

Claire McCardell

1900

1905 Born in Frederick, Maryland, USA

1910

1920

1925 Starts at Parson School of Design

1929 Works with designer Robert Turk

1931 Progresses to being the designer at Townley Frocks

1934 Launches range of interchangeable separates

1938 Joins Hattie Carnegie, working alongside Norman Norell

1942 Designs the denim 'Popover' dress

1940

1946 Unveils empire-waisted baby dress

1950

1953 Twenty-year retrospective at Frank Peris Gallery, Beverly Hills

1956 Publishes her memoir *What Shall I Wear?*

1958 Dies in New York, USA; posthumously inducted into Coty's Hall of Fame

1960

1970

1980

1990

'I don't think my work has ever been out of date, in that it was only ahead of its time.'

Charles James

1906–1978

UNITED KINGDOM

Ingenious, experimental and mathematical in approach, Charles James invented couture equations that have never been equalled. Balenciaga (p. 53) called him 'the world's best and only dressmaker', while Dior (p. 73) described James's talent simply as 'poetry'. A self-confessed perfectionist, and with a coterie of wealthy clients willing to pay handsomely and wait patiently, James thought nothing of spending a year reworking a sleeve. His dresses, which could weigh 8 kg (18 lb) and were often underpinned by a complex infrastructure of feather boning, nylon mesh, buckram and horsehair braid, occasionally veered towards the unwearable.

Commercial enterprise was alien to him. 'Nothing of worth is produced without the profound study of the structure reduced stage by stage to the minimum,' he said. The James signature involved folds, complicated understructures, pristine lines and dramatic silhouettes. He would often combine four fabrics in one garment, choosing them for their light-reflective qualities, drapery and structural properties.

Often hailed as the ultimate American couturier, James was actually an Englishman, but left England for Chicago in 1924. He headed for Long Island in 1928, setting up a studio in the Southampton district, where Diana Vreeland was one of his earliest clients. A year later, James relocated to England, opening a salon on Bruton Street, London. Hit by bankruptcy, he started selling his prototypes to retailers and manufacturers in Paris, London and New York, and in 1933 he reopened his London salon. That year James redesigned his

famous Taxi dress, which featured spiral seaming and appeared in advertisements for Lightning Zipp Fasteners. In October 1936 a series of dramatic coats and cloaks in whipcord, billiard-table felt and grosgrain was photographed for *Vogue*. Under the title 'Austere Exteriors' they were shot, surrealist style, in the window of Harrods by Cecil Beaton. Following his Paris couture debut in 1937, James flourished aesthetically, producing the Corselet dress, the Figure 8 skirt, and a gown fashioned from vintage grosgrain millinery ribbon.

The 1940s and 1950s were James's golden decades. His gowns were acquired not only by women who appreciated his extraordinary ability, but also by serious collectors and museums that were already recognizing his historic impact. By 1945, James was a permanent resident in the United States. Despite several forays into ready-to-wear, James's perfectionist streak caused financial setbacks. The 1960s were the beginning of the end for James. He moved into New York's Chelsea Hotel where he remained, relentlessly experimenting with proportion and shape until he died, penniless, aged 73.

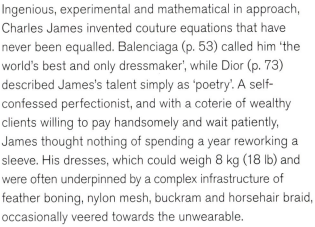

Opposite A peach silk faille and orange silk taffeta design which references the eighteenth century. 1948.

Overleaf This Cecil Beaton photograph from 1948 was commissioned to show off James's mastery of colour as well as his talent for cut and construction.

Charles James

1900

1906 — Born in Camberley, England

1910

— Attends Harrow School

1919 — Moves to Chicago to work in architecture department of utilities company

1924 — Opens a hat shop under the name Charles Boucheron, followed by a studio on Long Island
1926 — Relocates to London and opens salon on Bruton Street

1929 — Taxi dress features in advertisements for Lightning Zipp Fasteners

1933 — His gowns are photographed by Cecil Beaton for Vogue

1936 — Debuts Elizabeth Arden couture collection

1940

1944 — 'Decade of Design' exhibition of 45 garments held at Brooklyn Museum, commissioned by patron Millicent Rogers

1948 — Takes up residence at New York's Chelsea Hotel and meets illustrator Antonio Lopez, who

1950

1953 — draws his collections

1960

1970

— Dies penniless in the Chelsea Hotel, New York

1978 — 'The Genius of Charles James' exhibition takes place at Brooklyn Museum
1980

1982

1990

'I've made pretty things, but nothing perfect.'

Roger Vivier

1907–1998

FRANCE

A former sculptor, Roger Vivier was credited with inventing new heel shapes and creating breathtakingly beautiful shoes for the major Parisian couturiers. Employed by both Christian Dior (p. 73) and Yves Saint Laurent (p. 165), Vivier was originally discovered by Elsa Schiaparelli (p. 45). Recognizing his discerning eye for proportion and his ability to balance beauty with functionality, she commissioned him to design shoes for her collections. It was, however, his ten-year collaboration with Dior that made him famous. His outstanding talent earned him the titles 'the Fabergé of Footwear' and 'the Fragonard of the shoe'. Vivier commented: 'A shoe does not create fashion, but it can influence fashion.'

Vivier started his working life at the Théâtre de Belleville, Paris, but was steered towards design rather than drama, and found an apprenticeship at a relative's shoemaking workshop. His reputation quickly spread throughout the music hall fraternity, with the entertainers Mistinguett and Josephine Baker becoming his first clients. Vivier opened his own atelier in 1937. In addition to Dior and Schiaparelli, he also supplied custom-made shoes for Madame Grès (p. 69).

He emigrated to the United States during World War II, where he assisted photographer George Hoyningen-Huene, and even tried his hand at millinery. Returning to France, Vivier invented his landmark heel shape and perfect accompaniment to seamed stockings: the stiletto heel. Almost a decade later, in 1963, he employed the technique of aeronautical engineers in the construction of his seminal 'comma' heel.

With an incredible ability to adapt to the changing styles and demands of the key Parisian couturiers, Vivier worked with Cristóbal Balenciaga (p. 53), Guy Laroche, Emanuel Ungaro (p. 145), Pierre Balmain (p. 93), André Courrèges (p. 113), Nina Ricci and Yves Saint Laurent (p. 165). With Saint Laurent, Vivier's natural inclination towards decoration was temporarily brushed aside when he made his best-selling square-heeled pumps to complement Saint Laurent's 'Mondrian' collection in the mid-1960s.

By this time, Vivier's shoes were being coveted by celebrities on and off screen, including Gina Lollobrigida, Sophia Loren, Elizabeth Taylor, Jeanne Moreau and Ava Gardner. His Pilgrim pumps, worn by Catherine Deneuve in the film *Belle de Jour* (1967), became international bestsellers. Vivier's crowning moment was when he was commissioned to make gold kidskin sandals, the heels studded with 3,000 tiny garnets, for the coronation of Queen Elizabeth II.

Vivier continued to reinvent, refine and reinvigorate the concept of footwear throughout the 1970s and 1980s, culminating in a fiftieth-anniversary retrospective at Paris's Musée des Arts de la Mode. Christian Louboutin, who apprenticed with Vivier and assisted him with his retrospective, said of his style: 'His shoes were never just the "catch" of the moment, they were the definition of the moment.'

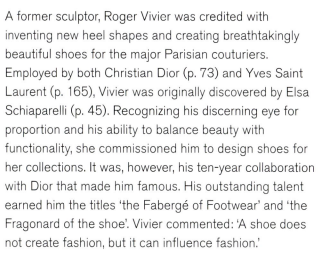

Opposite An atypical but timely magnified houndstooth patterned boot with square toe and block heel, 1966.

Opposite Extravagant embroidered evening shoe made by Vivier into an after-dark, ankle boot for Dior.

Above An early prototype, produced for German tannery Heyl-Liebenau in dyed and printed leather, shows an inventive use of texture, pattern and colour. 1934.

Above Jewelled evening shoes in silk satin, embroidered with beads, gilt thread, rhinestones and pink brilliants. 1958.

Below Silk satin evening shoe for Dior, with silk tulle overlay and central front layered decoration. Note the precisely chiselled pointed heel and toe. 1954.

Roger Vivier

- **1907** Born in Paris, France
- 1910
- **1920** Studies sculpture at Paris Ecole des Beaux-Arts
- **1925** Apprentices in shoe factories
- **1927** Works with French leather distributor Laboremus
- 1930
- **1936** Opens Vivier atelier at 22 rue Royale, Paris
- **1937** Moves to New York, employed by Delman
- **1940** Opens hat shop in Manhattan with Schiaparelli's former milliner, Suzanne Remy
- **1943** Returns to Paris, meeting Christian Dior
- **1947** Starts to make shoes for Dior's collections; commissioned to design a pair of jewelled pumps for Queen Elizabeth II's coronation
- 1950
- **1953** On Dior's death, Vivier begins collaborating with Yves Saint Laurent, Dior's successor
- **1957** Given a Neiman Marcus fashion award
- **1961** Designs thigh-high crocodile boots for Yves Saint Laurent as well as designs for Balenciaga, Courrèges and Ungaro
- **1963** Catherine Deneuve wears Vivier shoes for the film *Belle de Jour*
- **1967**
- 1970
- 1980
- **1988** Awarded the Officier dans l'Ordre des Arts et des Lettres by the French government
- 1990
- **1995** Opens boutique on rue de Grenelle, Paris
- **1998** Dies in Toulouse, France
- 2000

'One cannot understand the workings of haute couture without the realisation that it is based on publicity.'

Jacques Fath

1912–1954

FRANCE

'He makes you look like you have sex appeal, and believe me, that's important,' said *Harper's Bazaar* editor Carmel Snow of Fath's ability to add seductiveness to the fashion equation. A party animal par excellence who was the personification of glamour, elegance and joie de vivre, Fath appealed to the Parisian socialite, the American star and the international jet setter alike. *Life* magazine summed up the Fath ambience in 1949 by reporting: 'An atmosphere of glitter, chic, and perfumed excitement permeates both his personal and business affairs.' He was described as having 'the showy elegance of a character from a Cocteau play and the charm of an enfant terrible'. Fath, a natural showman, was self-educated in the art of stylish enhancement. Where many of his contemporaries were preoccupied with concocting new silhouettes, Fath was courting a coterie of new clients. His style is captured for posterity in the classic Powell and Pressburger film *The Red Shoes* (1948).

After completing military service, Fath enrolled in drama school, where he met Geneviève Boucher de la Bruyère, a former secretary to Chanel (p. 41), and started to educate himself in fashion design. With a small studio established, in 1937 Fath presented his first show consisting of 20 pieces, which was favourably received. Two years later he married his muse, Geneviève. Dressed in an asymmetrically draped dress and cape, she created a stir at the society racing event Grande Nuit de Longchamps, and *Vogue* reported about Fath: 'He is inspired. He has a vision. He will succeed.'

Drafted into the French Army as a gunner at the beginning of World War II, on his return he resumed business as usual. The Fath presentations continued to display his trademarks: fitted bodice, slender waistline, curvaceous hips. He had a penchant for dramatic detail, plunging necklines and exposed shoulders. His colour palette was equally sophisticated.

Still relatively unknown in the United States, Fath devised a charm offensive. He engaged the most fashionable women in Paris to wear his designs. In 1948, accompanied by his wife, Fath visited America, where he secured a deal to produce a ready-to-wear line with Seventh Avenue manufacturer Joseph Halpert. He was sufficiently famous to secure a commission to dress Hollywood darling Rita Hayworth in a blue crepe ensemble when she married Prince Aly Khan, and by 1950 Fath's name was firmly fixed on a global scale. In the year his career was cut tragically short, 1954, the American press were enthusiastically awaiting the next Fath collection, describing the 42-year-old as 'a fabulous young French designer who is out to make every woman look like a great beauty'.

Opposite A clever, inventive and insouciant approach to the sombre 1953 tailored suit, with interestingly placed pockets and looped collar with velvet tie.

Above When Rita Hayworth married Prince Aly Khan on the French Riviera in 1949, Fath was the couturier commissioned to make her ice blue wedding trousseau.

Opposite top Cascading, voluminous, layered, pleated evening coat. 1950s.

Opposite bottom Spotted silk fabric cut into a raglan-sleeved summer dress, high buttoning at the neck and flounced from the waist. 1940.

Jacques Fath · Paris

Mocles & Craveaux

Avril · 1949 · 31ᵉ Année · Nº 580.

Création de
Jacques Fath

Prix : **40** francs
IMPRIMÉ EN FRANCE

ÉDITIONS ÉDOUARD BOUCHERIT
10, RUE DE LA PÉPINIÈRE · PARIS

Jacques Fath

1910

1912 — Born in Maisons-Laffitte, France

1920

1928 — Studies business, law and bookkeeping
in Vincennes, France

1930

1937 — Presents first collection from his salon, debut
range of 20 pieces
Marries Geneviève Boucher de la
1939 — Bruyère, who wears a Fath outfit

Givenchy becomes Fath's assistant

1945 — Opens Paris boutique and establishes
Parfums Jacques Fath

1950 — Launches prêt a porter line, Jacques
Fath Université; dies in Paris, France

1954

1960

1970

1980

1990

2000

'Good fashion is evolution, not revolution.'

Pierre Balmain

1914–1982

FRANCE

'Not a bizarre note, but only beautiful clothes that you want to wear' – this was *Vogue*'s assessment of Pierre Balmain's Paris debut in 1945. Spoken about in the same breath as Christian Dior (p. 73), Jacques Fath (p. 89) and Cristóbal Balenciaga (p. 53), Balmain made a dazzling entrance into the couture arena. His meteoric rise to fame was not without reason: he already had an illustrious apprenticeship under his belt, having worked with notable designers Edward Molyneux, Lucien Lelong and Dior himself. Establishing his own atelier, Balmain was already on a par with the best. He was a trained architect, his eye attuned to proportion and scale. 'I often react as an architect, and think as an architect,' he was to observe retrospectively on his early training. 'There is certainly a huge amount of common ground between an architect and a couturier.'

Balmain's father, a drapery wholesaler, died when Pierre was 7 years old. His mother ran a boutique called Galeries Parisiennes and had a penchant for dressing her son in flamboyant outfits. Later, studying architecture but moonlighting as a fashion designer, Balmain sold sketches to Robert Piquet, then the artistic director of Redfern. After a brief stint in the French Air Force, Balmain returned to fashion, assisting Lelong and working alongside Dior. By 1943, Balmain had hit his stride, designing a black crepe afternoon dress entitled 'Little Profit' for Lelong that became a bestseller.

In October 1945 Balmain branched out on his own, opening his atelier, and one month later one of Balmain's dresses was being photographed by Cecil Beaton for *Vogue*. By December, Gertrude Stein was raving about Balmain's style and the Duchess of Windsor had become one of his first clients. The following year he was applauded for creating 'a new French style'. He created designs for the *Théâtre de la Mode*, made dresses for Helena Rubinstein and in 1947 launched his first fragrance, Elysées 64-83 (its name inspired by the atelier's telephone number), with a drawing by the famous fashion illustrator René Gruau.

In 1951 Balmain was reported as saying that 'hardly any American women are elegant', before opening a boutique in New York. His criticism did not affect business. On the contrary, he designed a white flannel wedding dress for Errol Flynn's third wife, Patrice Wymore, and a mink cape for Marlene Dietrich in *No Highway* (1951). He designed for both Broadway and the cinema, and in 1955 he won the Neiman Marcus Fashion Award. Two years before his death, in 1980, Balmain received a nomination for a Tony Award for Best Costume Design for the Broadway musical *Happy New Year*.

Opposite A swooping off-the-shoulder neckline secured at the base with a bow in floral print is paired with a button-through white ankle-length dress. 1953.

Left The eternally stylish Marlene Dietrich, who co-designed many of her stage costumes, wears a Balmain fur cape in *No Highway*, 1951.

Opposite This ingeniously constructed wrap coat, secured at the waist with a wide belt, combines abbreviated sleeves, shawl collar and back panel. 1958.

Pierre Balmain

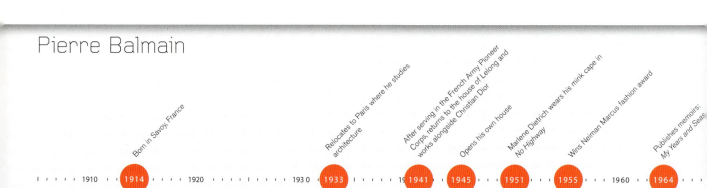

Born in Savoy, France

Relocates to Paris where he studies architecture

After serving in the French Army Pioneer Corps, returns to the house of Lelong and works alongside Christian Dior

Opens his own house

Marlene Dietrich wears his mink cape in *No Highway*

Wins Neiman Marcus fashion award

Publishes memoirs: *My Years and Seas*

1910　　1914　　1920　　1930　　1933　　19　　1941　　1945　　1951　　1955　　1960　　1964

Dies in Paris, France; the Dé d'Or
(Golden Thimble) posthumously awarded

'I don't know the first thing about fashion. I got my first job because of a pretty girl.'

Emilio Pucci

1914–1992

ITALY

Comprising vivid colour, geometric arrangements, architectural construction and psychedelic swirls, the Pucci print was the personification of 1950s Florentine chic. The charismatic Italian aristocrat who founded the company in 1947 kickstarted his career by designing skiwear and quickly progressed to producing separates for socialites. A former Italian Air Force pilot from one of Florence's oldest noble families, Emilio Pucci lived and worked in the fourteenth-century Palazzo Pucci in Florence for most of his life. With a lineage stretching back to the Renaissance, he had the perfect pedigree for a fashion brand that would appeal to the international jet set.

Surrounded by paintings by Botticelli and Leonardo da Vinci in his palazzo, Pucci was both creative and clinical in his approach to print. From a stock of 180,000 metres (600,000 feet) of fabric and a palette of approximately 80 colours, he selected up to 16 colours at a time. Among these were coral red, coral blue, geranium, almond green and 'Emilio pink'. His talent was not only for tonal inventiveness and precise line but in placing the pattern in the correct proportions.

Emilio Pucci was an accomplished sportsman who began designing purely by chance. While skiing in Switzerland, Pucci met *Harper's Bazaar* photographer Toni Frissel, who asked to photograph his ski outfit. When she discovered he had designed it she asked him to design a women's capsule collection, which appeared in the Winter 1948 issue of *Harper's Bazaar*. The design, which combined stretch with a sleek silhouette, caused a sensation. He set up his studio on Capri and initially produced a swimwear line. He progressed to silk scarves, blouses and silk-jersey shift dresses.

By the early 1950s the Pucci name was international, and the ensuing decade saw it underlined by a new celebrity following, which included Marilyn Monroe, Jacqueline Kennedy and Sophia Loren. In 1961 *Time* magazine reported on the synthetics revolution in fashion, naming Pucci as the 'Undisputed master of the smashable dress' and *Vogue* wrote that his 'six-ounce stretch silks are used in everything from ball gowns to bikinis'. The following year Pucci launched his first haute couture collection and in 1964 he was credited by *Vogue* as 'one of the first to make women look really enchanting in pants'. After Emilio Pucci's death in 1992 his daughter Laudomia took over. 'The most precious thing my father left me was not his archive but his spirit,' she said.

Opposite Inspired by a visit to Lake Tanganyika, Pucci created this 'barracano' silk hooded cover-up with psychedelic patterning. c. 1965.

Below Shown in the Florentine Pitti Palace, this daring, sleeveless evening dress pattern is split into quarters. 1967.

Opposite Model Suzy Parker wearing a signature print shirt paired with capri pants, a combination which was also a favourite of Marilyn Monroe. 1953.

Emilio Pucci

Born in Naples, Italy

Member of the Italian team in the Winter Olympics

Receives Doctorate in Political Science from the University of Florence

His skiwear is spotted and photographed on the slopes by Toni Frissel

First fashion show with sportswear and printed scarves

Debuts signature silk jersey dress; receives the Neiman Marcus fashion award

Presents his first couture collec 'Reigning Beauties', inspired
Jacqueline Kennedy

1910 · 1914 · 1920 · 1930 · 1932 · 194 · 1941 · 1947 · 195 · 1951 · 1954 · 1960 · 1962 · · ·

Designs Vespa motorcyle for Fiat

Receives a knighthood from the Italian government

Dies in Florence, Italy, having retired only two years earlier; his daughter Laudomia takes over the company

| 1977 | 1980 | 1982 | 1990 | 1992 | 2000 | 2010 |

'Missoni? It's a lifestyle,
more than fashion.'

Ottavio & Rosita Missoni

Ottavio Missoni 1921–2013, CROATIA

Rosita Jelmini b. 1931, ITALY

'Colour? What can I say? I like comparing colour to music,' said Ottavio Missoni. 'Only seven notes and yet innumerable melodies have been composed.' The epitome of sublime simplicity, the Missoni signature pivoted on a multicoloured zig-zag and kaleidoscopic stripe. Taking a mercurial palette and merging it with an artisan attitude, the Italian duo transformed the knitwear industry in a way defined by Rosita Missoni as 'lifestyle more than fashion'. In 1973 the *New York Times* declared that 'Missoni's knitted clothes have become international status symbols, like Vuitton bags and Gucci shoes'.

Founder Ottavio 'Tai' Missoni was born in Dubrovnik, Croatia, his father an Italian sea captain, his mother a Croatian countess. An accomplished athlete of international standing, after the war Missoni set up a workshop in Trieste with his friend Giorgio Oberweger making wool tracksuits, which would be worn by the Italian Olympic team. Ottavio's Italian wife-to-be, Rosita Jelmini, was the daughter of a family of shawl makers. After their marriage in 1953, they set up a small knitwear workshop in Gallarate in Lombardy, northern Italy, and in 1958 presented their first collection of striped shirt dresses, which sold to upmarket Italian department store La Rinascente.

Four years later, Missoni inadvertently invented the brand's signature zig-zag pattern. 'We could only do stripes,' remembered Rosita. 'Then we started doing horizontal and vertical and little by little added more complicated stitches, plaids and jacquards.' Legendary Italian *Vogue* editor Anna Piaggi began to promote the Missonis, later stating, 'They really started a knitwear revolution'. After a fortuitous meeting with French stylist Emmanuelle Khanh, Missoni showed at the Pitti Palace in

April 1967. The presentation caused a sensation after Rosita instructed the models to remove their obtrusive underwear but the knitwear then became unintentionally translucent under the lights. The resultant coverage made the Missoni name. Their designs were subsequently championed by Diana Vreeland. On seeing their collection her reaction was definitive: 'Look! Who said that only colours exist? There are also tones.'

The early 1970s saw the Missoni name at its height. Bloomingdale's department store in New York opened an in-store Missoni boutique. Pinpointed by *Vogue*, the Missoni style was christened 'the put-together look', with the magazine writing: 'Count on Missoni to give you a sweater you never owned before.'

As the 1980s dawned, Missoni diversified. Missoni Home was launched, with the pattern adorning everything from a scented candle to a crochet-knit bikini. Tai Missoni, once named one of the most elegant men in the world, undertook other projects, the most ambitious of which were Missoni Hotels.

Opposite Missoni edged iridescent knitwear with luxury by elongating proportions and pairing patterns, and adding a cloche knitted hat. 1975.

Above A revealing chevron, lurex cardigan, unbuttoned to the waist with evening trousers, also lurex. Spring/ Summer 2004.

Opposite No longer confined to daywear, eveningwear or occasionwear, variations of the signature pattern are applied to beachwear, 2002.

Ottavio & Rosita Missoni

1921 Ottavio Missoni born in Dubrovnik, Croatia

1931 Rosita Jelmini born in Golasecca, Italy

1940

1947 On leaving the army, Ottavio produces wool tracksuits to be worn by the Italian Olympic Team

1950

1953 Ottavio and Rosita marry and set up Maglificio Jolly studio in Gallarate, Italy

1958 Launch of Missoni garments sold to Italian department store La Rinascente

1960

1963 Missoni signature of zig-zag motifs and viscose blends developed

1967 Debut of Missoni collection sold in Paris

1970 Missoni boutique opens in Bloomingdales, New York

1976 Missoni boutique opens in Milan

1978 25-year retrospective of Missoni clothes staged at New York's Whitney Museum

1980

1990

1994 Missonologia exhibition opens in Florence

1998 M Missoni line launched

2000

2009 First Missoni hotel opens in Edinburgh

2013 Ottavio Missoni dies in Sumirago, Italy

'The clothes I prefer are those I invent for a life that doesn't exist yet – the world of tomorrow.'

Pierre Cardin

b. 1922

ITALY

The stereotypical fashion designer achieves notoriety via a headline-grabbing garment. Pierre Cardin became infamous for unashamedly exploiting his name: his 1991 biography was appropriately entitled *The Man Who Became A Label*. When the Pierre Cardin company celebrated its sixtieth anniversary in 2010, there were more than 1,000 products, the minority fashion-related.

From the outset, Cardin was a futurist in the truest sense of the word. Not only did he advocate a Space Age dress code, but he created a sartorial business model that has become the template for the twenty-first-century fashion industry. Half a century ago, Cardin built his empire on a pioneering principle – that a designer name associated with clothing could successfully be applied to virtually any type of consumer product. In Cardin's case this meant everything from a hairdryer to a frying pan. 'Everything is Pierre Cardin,' he said in 2003. 'I can wake up in the morning and shave with one of my razors, use my own aftershave and dress in Pierre Cardin from my tie to my pants to my shirt. Everything in my house is Pierre Cardin too – even what I eat, because I have a range of food products too.'

Cardin was born Pietro Cardin in the Italian province of Treviso in 1922, but was brought up in France. In 1939 he was apprenticed to a tailor in Vichy, but moved to Paris in 1945. On the recommendation of a friend he joined the atelier of couturier Jeanne Paquin, and then of Elsa Schiaparelli (p. 45). Having tried unsuccessfully three times to secure a position with his hero, Cristóbal Balenciaga (p. 53), he joined Christian Dior (p. 73) in

1946, working on the seminal New Look of 1947. By the age of 28, Cardin had set up his own label, in 1953 presenting his first haute couture show and in 1959 unveiling his first ready-to-wear collection – the first couturier to do so. The following year he presented his first men's couture collection.

Cardin was as fascinated by accountancy as he was with aesthetics, and by the 1970s diversification – not fashion design – became his preoccupation. Having signed his first licensing contract for men's shirts and ties in 1959, a decade later he turned his hand to transportation, restyling Cadillacs, private jets and boats. Always with his eye on new and emerging markets, in 1981 Cardin became the first European designer to open a showroom in China. He then launched in the Soviet Union, later saying, 'I didn't invent glasnost or perestroika, but I'm glad to have been a bit player in these great events.' In later life, he hit the headlines not for his saleable ideas but for his architectural interventions.

Opposite Equally influenced by space age and futuristic architecture, Cardin creates a fur-trimmed helmet and button-through coat with cut-out panels. 1968.

Below Insect-like eyewear and shift dresses with stand-up collar and central circular detail in contrasting colourways. 1970.

Opposite Wearable, conventional dresses in four shades where the hemline is below, rather than above, the knee. 1968.

Pierre Cardin

- 1920
- **1922** Born near Venice, Italy

- 1930

- **1936** Begins his fashion career as a tailor's assistant

- 1940

- **1945** Moves to Paris. Studies architecture and works first with Paquin then Schiaparelli; meets Jean Cocteau and Christian Bérard with whom he makes costumes and masks

- **1950** Creates his fashion house on the rue Richepanse, Paris

- **1953** Present first haute couture collection and the following year launches the bubble dress

- First menswear collection

- **1960** Launch of his first children's collection

- **1966** Opens his theatre, Espace Pierre Cardin, which houses an art gallery, restaurant and private cinema

- **1970** Opens his first design boutique in Paris

- **1975** Celebration of 30 years of his work at the Metropolitan Museum, New York

- **1980** Appointed a UNESCO goodwill ambassador; presents fashion show in Moscow before 200,000 guests

- **1991** Retrospective of 50 years of his work in Paris

- **1997**

- 2000

- 2010

'Baring breasts seemed logical in a period of freer attitudes, freer minds, the emancipation of women.'

Rudi Gernreich

1922–1985

AUSTRIA

'Fashion isn't tragedy, it's entertainment,' announced Rudi Gernreich in the Swinging Sixties, underlining his intention to bring showmanship to the American arena. A natural performer, a former dancer, a gay activist and a designer with a flair for public relations, he secured the cover of *Time* magazine in 1967. The prestigious publication, which had previously featured Christian Dior (p. 73), described Gernreich as 'the most way-out, far-ahead designer in the US'. Gernreich was an advocate of unisex dressing and viewed clothing as a form of social experiment. His muse, Peggy Moffitt, who was married to Gernreich's favourite photographer, William Claxton, and modelled his most groundbreaking creations, said: 'I thought he was a total genius. He was 30 years ahead of his time.'

An Austrian-born agent provocateur, Gernreich lost his father, a hosiery manufacturer, when he was only 8 years old. At 16, Gernreich fled Austria with his mother and settled in Los Angeles, joining Lester Horton's modern dance troupe as both costume designer and dancer. By 1943, Gernreich had started freelancing as a textile designer, then headed to New York in 1949 to work for a coat and suit company. In 1952 he opened his own design studio. With Vidal Sassoon's five-point haircut as a finishing touch, Gernreich's style was stark, synthetic and psychedelic.

According to Moffitt, wealth was never the prime motivation for Gernreich. 'Money was not important. It was always to be first.' He achieved his ultimate act of notoriety in 1964 with his 'monokini', a swimsuit that left the breasts exposed. 'Rudi thought the bathing suit was

over. The next logical thing was for a woman just to wear a bikini bottom.' He followed this with the translucent 'No-Bra Bra', which – pulled over the head rather than fastening at the back – became a bestseller. Gernreich then capitalized on his fame, producing a line of complementary lingerie, hosiery, accessories, cosmetics and perfume.

At the pinnacle of his career, in 1968, Gernreich suddenly announced he was taking a year off 'to think things through'. 'I'm totally unconcerned with skirt lengths,' he had said in 1966. 'They are not the issue. The issue is flying to the moon, killing men in Vietnam. Life isn't pretty. Clothes can't be pretty little things.' This decision to take time-out proved to be a catalyst for change. In 1970 he produced military safari clothes complete with dog tags and machine guns. Two years' later the *New York Times* reported: 'Rudi Gernreich opened the Rites of Spring on Seventh Avenue yesterday with a laugh. He sent a mannequin into his showroom in a dress with four sleeves.'

Opposite Gernreich's muse and model Peggy Moffitt wears a sleeveless mini dress with see-through central plastic strip from the Spring/Summer 1968 collection.

Rudi Gernreich

Born in Vienna, Austria

Family moves to the US

Studies art at Los Angeles Art Center School

Produces first capsule clothing collection

Wins American Sportswear Design award from *Sports Illustrated*, Men's jackets designed by Gernreich appear in *Life* magazine

Produces the 'monoki and the 'No-Bra B

1910   1920 1922   1930   1938 9 1941   1949 0   1956   1960   1964

Opposite Model Rose McWilliams wears Gernreich's original topless bathing suit, the 'monokini', at a rooftop fashion show. June 1964.

Right A woollen, military-style tunic from the early 1970s, which also resembles safari clothing.

'I design for women and however much I try to be intuitive and understanding, inevitably there are times when I feel and react like a man.'

André Courrèges

b. 1923

FRANCE

Fresh from seeing his Space Age vision unveiled in the autumn of 1963, *Vogue* summed up the Courrèges signature thus: 'Courrèges is tomorrow – begun today.' His futuristic presentation at the Paris Couture show was accessorized with go-go boots and Inuit goggles, and caused such an impact that the magazine commissioned a photo shoot with Irving Penn. 'Courrèges has perfected the straight line, bringing everything close to the body,' reported *Vogue*. 'His tailoring is without peer, subtle, correct, and modern.'

The Courrèges story began with both André and his partner Cocqueline Barrière securing a loan from Cristóbal Balenciaga (p. 53) in order to open their own couture house in Paris. Both had worked with Balenciaga, and Courrèges had been there for a decade before daring to branch out on his own. The first show in 1961 was warmly received, but it was the seminal collection three years later that propelled the Courrèges name into fashion history.

Running parallel with what was happening in London, Courrèges claimed, along with Mary Quant, to be the originator of the miniskirt. Both designers promoted what fashion editor Diana Vreeland called the 'youthquake', a modern aesthetic of high-tech materials, slick shapes, abbreviated hemlines and adolescent faces. Inspired by the architecture of Le Corbusier, and coupled with his own impeccable couture credentials, Courrèges was able to combine modernity with a masterly approach to proportion. Despite having served an apprenticeship in Balenciaga's rarefied atelier, Courrèges was fascinated by functionality, sportswear and freedom of movement. He mixed luxury with logic, for example incorporating a front slit at the bottom of a pair of trousers to enable

them to break over the boot. Grabbing the headlines and creating waves on both sides of the Atlantic, Courrèges's inventions were met with disdain by the old guard. Chanel dismissed his style, saying he was trying to 'destroy women by covering up their figures and turning them into little girls'.

Courrèges did not waver from his initial vision. In 1967 he introduced a more affordable, diffusion line called 'Couture Future'. Andy Warhol, an admirer, applauded the streamlined look, which lent itself to uniformity. 'Courrèges clothes are so beautiful,' he said. 'Everyone should look the same, dressed in silver. Silver merges into everything. Costumes should be worn during the day with lots of makeup.' Throughout the 1960s and 1970s Courrèges continued to stick with his original concept, with the *New York Times* stating in 1975: 'For Courrèges, it's always the 1960s, the time of the early explorations of space, when his Space Age clothes captured the fashion consciousness of the world.'

Twenty years later, when Courrèges stepped down from the day-to-day running of the business, his design signature remained unchanged: 'My clothes are still very clean and devoid of any ornamentation.'

Opposite Sleeveless top with low-cut armholes and slim trousers with elongated side seams in ecru, presented as part of the widely copied Spring/ Summer 1965 collection.

Overleaf This 1968 futuristic show featured helmets, capes, moon boots and a two-tone line-up of A-line silhouettes accessorized with flat shoes.

André Courrèges

- 1920
- **1923** Born in Pau, France; educated at the National School of Civil Engineering
- 1930
- 1940
- **1944** Serves an Air Force Pilot at Aix-en-Provence
- **1946** Studies fashion in Paris
- 1950
- **1961** Borrows money from Balenciaga to found his own couture house with his wife
- **1964** Presents seminal Space Age ensemble
- **1967** Launches 'Couture Future', an affordable line comprising 15 looks
- **1970** Enters the mass market with his 'Hyperbole' collection
- **1973** Menswear line 'Courrèges Homme' introduced
- 1980
- 1990
- **1994** Iconic designs from past collections reintroduced
- 2000
- **2003** Marc Jacobs pays homage to Courrèges in his collection
- **2011** Celebrates 50 years in business
- 2010

'Fabric is where it all begins.
The preamble to inspiration.'

Hubert de Givenchy

b. 1927

FRANCE

A French aristocrat of statuesque proportions and impeccable taste, Hubert de Givenchy was the perfect choreographer for the persona of Audrey Hepburn. 'His are the only clothes in which I am myself,' she said. 'He is far more than a couturier, he is a creator of a personality.' Givenchy's watchwords – restraint, perfection, understatement, refinement – were directly reflected in his design signature. He defined an era where less was more and elegance was instinctive. Givenchy's mentor and all-time hero was Cristóbal Balenciaga (p. 53), who gave him a clinical white coat that he always wore at the end of each show.

Born Count Hubert James Marcel Taffin de Givenchy in 1927, he studied at the Collège Félix Faure in Beauvais, followed by the École nationale supérieure des Beaux-Arts in Paris. In 1945 he became an apprentice at Jacques Fath (p. 89), followed by design training in the salons of Robert Piguet, Lucien Lelong and legendary Surrealist Elsa Schiaparelli (p. 45). He opened his own house in 1952 on the rue Alfred de Vigny, launching his vision of Parisian sophistication, pioneering the idea of separates and presenting the 'Bettina' blouse, named after model Bettina Graziani, who was also head of Givenchy's public relations.

Initially invited to dress Audrey Hepburn in *Sabrina* (1954), Givenchy went on to devise her wardrobe for *Funny Face* (1957) and transformed her into an icon of chic for the cinematic adaptation of Truman Capote's *Breakfast at Tiffany's* (1961). Theirs was a meeting of minds, with Givenchy designing her wardrobe both on and off camera. 'They not only thrilled me but gave me so much confidence,' Hepburn said of Givenchy's clothes. 'I've worked in them, I've played in them, I've borrowed them, I've bought them.' Hepburn also promoted Givenchy's first fragrance, L'Interdit, in 1957, and as the

face of Givenchy, his clientele became an assembly of the eternally chic: Jacqueline Kennedy, Maria Callas, Marlene Dietrich, Greta Garbo, Grace Kelly, Babe Paley and the Duchess of Windsor.

The debonair Givenchy, a customer of Huntsman tailors on Savile Row, and simply called 'Le Grand' in fashion circles, was named in the International Best Dressed List Hall of Fame in 1970. In 1992, Le Palais Galliera staged a visual celebration of Givenchy's 40 years in fashion.

Gone from the fashion world but not forgotten, Givenchy now lives predominantly at his country estate just outside Paris. A connoisseur of sculpture, furniture and works of art, he was employed by the auction house Christie's as its president in France. In July 2010, Givenchy was coaxed into making a rare public appearance, giving a talk at the Oxford Union. Two years later he was the focus of a film entitled *Monsieur Hubert de Givenchy*, launched at the Montreal Museum of Fine Arts. Musing on fashion today, he said: 'I loved my job and was lucky to do it in the time of real couture. We would dress women to make them beautiful. Now they are sold bags and shoes.'

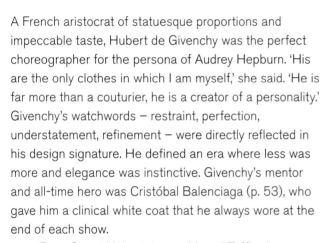

Opposite Givenchy defined Audrey Hepburn's gamine look on and off stage. Here she is shown in 1959.

1920

1927 Born in Beauvais, France

1930

1940

1944 Moves to Paris, enrolling at the École des
Beaux-Arts; on graduating, becomes assistant
to designer Jacques Fath

1950

1952 Founds House of Givenchy in Paris
1953 Meets his lifelong muse, Audrey Hepburn
1954 Debut of his Pret a Porter collection

Creation of the Givenchy 'sack' silhouette

1957 Dresses Hepburn in *Breakfast at Tiffany's*

1961

Launch of menswear line 'Gentleman Givenchy'

1970

1973

1980

Sold his label to LVMH; succeeded by John
1988 Galliano, then Alexander McQueen

1990

Retires from fashion design

1995

2000

2010

Above Constructed from cotton shirting
and featuring ruffled sleeves embroidered
with eyelets, the 'Bettina' blouse featured
in the couture collection of 1952.

Opposite Produced in the same year
Givenchy first met Balenciaga, this suit,
comprising voluminous printed skirt and
black silk satin jacket, is a sophisticated
meeting of day and eveningwear. 1953.

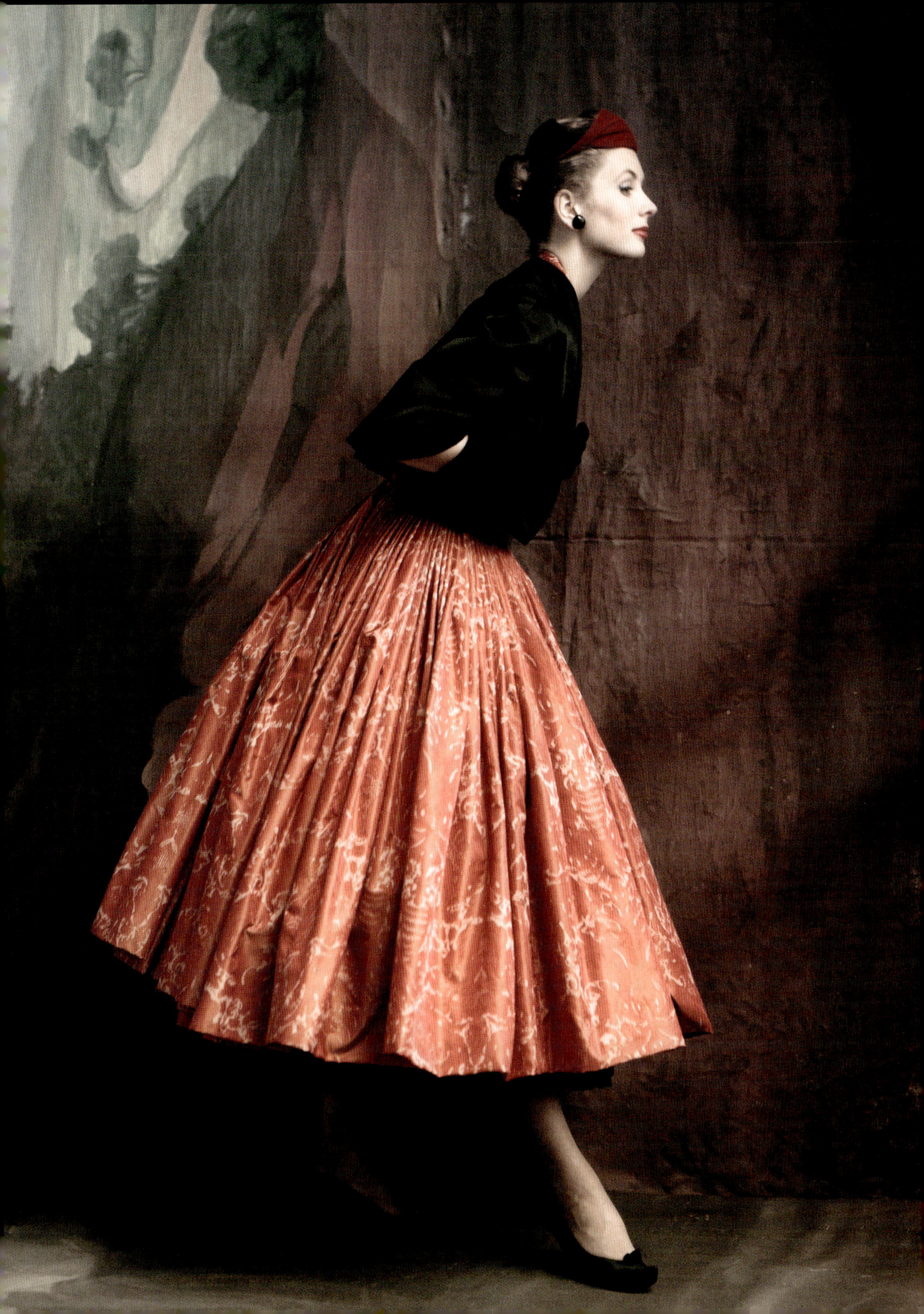

'Clothes should be as interesting on the inside as on the outside.'

Geoffrey Beene

1927–2004

UNITED STATES

Creator of the kind of designs that are virtually impossible to date, Geoffrey Beene invented an experimental style that stood outside mainstream American fashion. His philosophy was not based on seasonal whims but on eternal anatomical principles. As *Vogue* was to state in 1988, 'He is the most original, idiosyncratic and autonomous creator in his field.' Beene himself once said, 'I hate trends.'

The foundation for all his ideas was the female form. Born in Louisiana and having begun training as a medical student at Tulane University, after a year Beene swapped his stethoscope for a pair of dressmaking scissors. For the duration of his fashion career, a woman's body became the basis for his design signature. Beene listed his favourite areas for accentuation as the nape of the neck, the upper arm, the arch of the foot, the ankle, the back side of the hip and the small of the back – which he described as 'still life distilled'.

On leaving Tulane, Beene studied fashion design in Los Angeles, Paris and New York before working in Manhattan's garment district. Paris, remembered Beene, 'changed everything for me'. In 1963, Geoffrey Beene Inc. was formed, and his first collection made the cover of *Vogue*. The following year he was the recipient of the first of a lifetime total of eight Coty awards. From the beginning, his collections had the hallmarks of an uncompromising designer who understood his art. 'Fabric dictates,' declared Beene, who managed to combine the often contradictory qualities of extreme luxury and effortless ease. Beene's signature included geometric shapes, architectural lines, spots, stripes, shoestring straps and slices of translucency. He had a penchant for triangles. He became famous for reworking the bolero, putting a new perspective on sportswear and promoting the jumpsuit as a viable alternative to the traditional ballgown. Although Beene became known for a neutral palette, he was not averse to colour.

Beene's breakthrough moment – the point at which his name became known on a global scale – came in 1967, when he was asked to design the wedding dress for Lynda Bird Johnson (daughter of the then-president). By 1971 Beene had spread his corporate wings, commercializing the Beene brand into a 'Beene Bag' diffusion line and extending his label into furs, jewellery and shoes. In 1976 he became the first ready-to-wear designer from the United States to show in Italy. Invitations followed to present his collections in Rome, Paris, Brussels and Vienna. Preferring to look resolutely forward rather than back, Beene reluctantly agreed to a 25-year retrospective. 'A retrospective is like sailing into the sunset and I'm not,' he said. 'If I am then I'm not saying goodbye, I'm waving hello.'

Opposite Undulations, understatement and an innate understanding of the human anatomy is shown in this evening dress engineered in sheer and matte fabrics. 1992.

Opposite A shimmering, sequinned evening take on the all-American football shirt which led to a Coty award. 1977.

Right Structured, raglan-sleeved silk gazar coat over elegant horizontally striped silk pyjamas. 1981.

Below A rare example of Beene's talent for fluidity in a paisley printed crepe de Chine dress, slipping seductively off the shoulder. 1977.

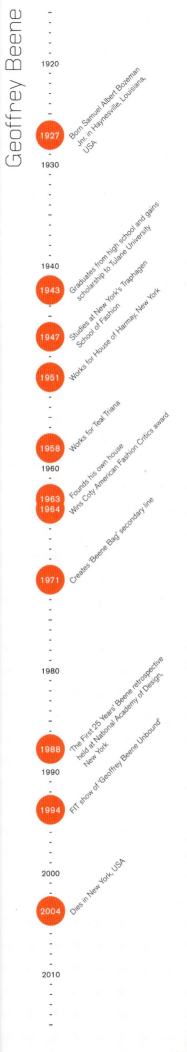

Geoffrey Beene

- 1920
- **1927** Born Samuel Albert Bozeman Jnr. in Haynesville, Louisiana, USA
- 1930
- 1940
- **1943** Graduates from high school and gains scholarship to Tulane University
- **1947** Studies at New York's Traphagen School of Fashion
- **1951** Works for House of Harmay, New York
- **1958** Works for Teal Triana
- 1960
- **1963** Founds his own house
- **1964** Wins Coty American Fashion Critics award
- **1971** Creates 'Beene Bag' secondary line
- 1980
- **1988** 'The First 25 Years' Beene retrospective held at National Academy of Design, New York
- 1990
- **1994** FIT show of 'Geoffrey Beene Unbound'
- 2000
- **2004** Dies in New York, USA
- 2010

'The clothes in themselves do not make a statement. The woman makes a statement and the dress helps.'

Jean Muir

1928–1995

UNITED KINGDOM

Preferring to be called a dressmaker rather than a fashion designer, Jean Muir was dubbed *la reine de la robe* in France. A staunch disciplinarian, perfectionist and dedicated craftswoman, Muir started her business in the Swinging Sixties, but her sensibility was a world apart from the era in which she made her name. 'I am not particularly hung up on clothes,' she declared. 'I am hung up on the making of them.' Internationally regarded as on a par with Madame Grès (p. 69), Coco Chanel (p. 41) and Madeleine Vionnet (p. 29), Jean Muir was one of the first designers to apply couture standards to ready-to-wear. Her primary materials of choice – cashmere, wool crepe, matte jersey, and suede – were given the Muir treatment, a process that paired understated elegance with subtle body-consciousness. 'She had real style that you could recognize instantly and which was unique,' said Jean Paul Gaultier (p. 249).

'I'm told I am extremely creative but I am also an enormous pragmatist,' observed Muir, attributing her acute colour sense and natural straightforwardness to her Scottish ancestry. As a child Muir revealed a talent for making, being able to knit, sew and embroider by the age of six. She left school at 17 and secured a stockroom job at Liberty & Co, which proved both a catalyst and a springboard for Muir's career. Although she had no formal training, she was given the opportunity to rise through the ranks and develop her design talent.

From Liberty, she progressed to Jaeger, where she developed the Young Jaeger fashion label, in 1962 branching out under the name Jane & Jane. She left in 1966 to launch Jean Muir Ltd. From the outset, the Jean Muir look was consistently contemporary, merging couture touches with affordable price tags. 'Quite immodestly, it was actually the beginning of what is now called designer ready-to-wear' she said. Although associated primarily with black and navy blue, Muir was, by her own admission, 'mad about colour', and worked closely with fabric mills and dyers to achieve the precise shade she had in mind. Her client list encompassed the theatrical, artistic and literary worlds.

In the same way that Muir's customers reflected a mix of artistic disciplines, she never confined herself to fashion. Elected Master of the Faculty of Royal Designers for Industry in 1993, Muir felt at ease with world-class illustrators, sculptors, architects and, particularly, engineers. 'She was just the best,' said Mary Quant (p. 153), one of Muir's contemporaries from the 1960s. 'People will go on wearing those dresses for years.'

Opposite House model and fervent Jean Muir fan Joanna Lumley in a fluid matte jersey ensemble photographed in Muir's all-white London flat in 1975.

Jean Muir

Opposite Commissioned as part of Australia's bicentennial celebrations, this pure wool collection was inspired by the Great Barrier Reef. 1988.

Above Multiple rows of exacting stitching, particularly present on the cuff, and the use of wool crepe were two Muir hallmarks. 1970.

Below A selection of tailored pieces in leather suede and wool crepe exhibited at the National Museum of Scotland's tribute 'Jean Muir: A Fashion Icon', 2008.

1920

1928 — Born in London, England

1930

1940

1950 — Employed by Liberty & Co. while studying fashion drawing at St. Martin's School of Art

1956 — Designs for Jaeger and develops Young Jaeger

1960

1962 — Establishes own label called 'Jane & Jane'; wins Dress of the Year Award at Fashion Museum, Bath

1966 — Founds Jean Muir Ltd

1970

1972 — Elected to the Royal Designers for Industry

1981 — Honorary Doctorate from the Royal College of Art

1984 — Awarded a CBE

1988 — Wins the Australian Bicentennial Wool Award

1991 — Jean Muir Ltd celebrates 25 years in business

1995 — Dies in London, England

2000

2010

'The key to my collections is sensuality.'

Sonia Rykiel

b. 1930

FRANCE

Once voted one of the world's most elegant women, flame-haired Sonia Rykiel is known internationally as the Queen of Knits. She hates the word 'feminine', loves the idea of androgyny and has developed a look that is distinctly off-centre. 'It's the ambiguity which is disturbing and attractive,' she said. 'The women friends I am closest to somehow have this masculine side to them. They shove their hands in their pockets when they walk. I love that side.' Stating that seduction is always at the core of her design signature, Rykiel's fashion philosophy is essentially French: definite, uncompromising and original. 'As soon as one has found one's look, one's shape, one does not need to alter it too much.'

Appealing to intelligent and intellectual women, Rykiel's seriousness about her craft belies a healthy sense of humour. She is partial to intarsia, quirky detailing, flirtatious touches that counterpoint the tomboyish element that is often present in her collections. The designer she most admires is Jean Paul Gaultier (p. 249).

Without any formal training, Sonia Flis, who was brought up in what she describes as a 'very bourgeois family', discovered her love of art through an uncle who was a painter. As a teenager, she worked as a window dresser at the Grande Maison de Blanc in Paris and, on marrying Sam Rykiel in 1953, took over management of his parents' boutique, Laura. When Rykiel searched for, but could not find, clothes that would suit her newly pregnant status, she made maternity wear.

Within a decade, Rykiel had sufficient confidence in her design abilities to launch her own company. Her first flagship store was forced to close owing to the student riots of 1968, but she persevered and in 1969 opened a shop within a shop in the Galeries Lafayette. Applauded for her sinuous line and particular expertise with knits

and jerseys, Rykiel was included by *Vogue* in its 1972 list of '12 top designers in European ready-to-wear'.

Rykiel saw menswear as a natural progression, and by 1976 was designing men's sweaters. This new direction created a sea change in her ethos. In the same year the *New York Times* reported 'Sonia Rykiel declared … that fashion does not exist, that it is, in fact, out of style'. In the collection Rykiel showed an evening shift with the word 'MODE' embroidered on the front – but crossed out. Claiming that she had taken clothes 'as far as they can go', Rykiel started to deconstruct fashion, exposing seams, turning outfits inside out.

Since the 1960s, Sonia Rykiel's signature has been the unexpected, verging on the eccentric. 'It's the attitude of never exactly perfect,' she told André Leon Talley of American *Vogue*. 'I like a Parisian kind of elegance: an attitude of nonchalance and irreverence.'

Opposite Essentially French, perennially feminine, always with a suggestion of androgyny – whatever the collection, luxurious knits are ever present. 1975.

Above Signature striped, dolman-sleeved knitwear, accessorized with sailor berets, show variations on a nautical theme. 1986.

Opposite Definitive, striking intarsia knits in delicate yarns are translated into both sweaters and long-sleeved dresses in this 1970 collection.

Sonia Rykiel

1920

1930 — Born Sonia Flis in Neuilly, France

1940

1948 — Employed as a window dresser at the Grande Maison de Blanc, Paris

1950 — Marries Sam Rykiel, owner of a boutique

1953 — Starts designing sweaters while pregnant with her first child

1960

1962 — Opens a shop in Galeries Lafayette

1969

1970

1980 — Voted one of the world's most elegant women

1987 — Launch of 'Sonia Rykiel Enfant'; '20 Ans de Mode' retrospective

1989 — Creation of Rykiel Homme

1990 — Collaborates with music impresario Malcolm McLaren on his song *Who The Hell Is Sonia Rykiel?*

1995

2000 — Launches an in-store boutique in department store Henri Bendel, New York

2005 — Collaborates with H&M on two collections including underwear

2009

'I like light, colour, luminosity. I like things full of colour and vibrant.'

Oscar de la Renta

1932–2014

DOMINICAN REPUBLIC

'Any great designer will have a point of view, a look and a signature. That's what Oscar has,' said *Vogue* editor Anna Wintour. 'Oscar's success is wrapped up in his incredible joie de vivre.' A party animal with a winning smile and charming personality, de la Renta was the couturier of choice for New York's elite. Dubbed 'the Sultan of Suave', for more than half a century he was mingling with and creating clothes for the upper echelons of Manhattan society. De la Renta's look was not revolutionary, extraordinary or the kind to warrant detailed analysis. His clothes were simply exquisite examples of female flattery.

The de la Renta style evolved as a consequence of his close proximity to his customer. 'I have watched women crossing barriers that at one time were unthinkable,' he said, naming Chanel (p. 41) as the designer who made the greatest impact. 'She really created the modern woman of today. She was the most creative and innovative designer of the twentieth century.'

Born and brought up in the Dominican Republic, de la Renta studied painting at the Academy of San Fernando in Madrid, Spain. An accomplished artist, he became fascinated with fashion design. On showing his portfolio of drawings, he secured a position 'picking up pins' at Balenciaga (p. 53) in Madrid, and later assisting Antonio del Castillo at Lanvin (p. 21) in Paris. A fortuitous meeting with Elizabeth Arden in New York led to a job offer, which, on the advice of Diana Vreeland, he accepted despite also being offered a position at Christian Dior (p. 73). 'Go to Arden because you will make your reputation faster,' advised Vreeland. 'She is not a designer but she will promote you.' In 1963, de la Renta relocated to Manhattan and quickly came to the attention of *Women's Wear Daily*, which described him as a 'slim, suave, stripe-suited Paris importation'.

Two years later de la Renta had moved on, designing for the Jane Derby company before forming his own line in 1965. He went on to win Coty awards for his 'Road of Spices' collection and 'Belle Epoque' show. By 1970 he was appealing to a younger audience and the company continued to grow and diversify, in 1989 being worth half a billion dollars, with three fragrances and 45 licences. In 1992 de la Renta became the first American since Mainbocher (p. 49) to head a Parisian couture house when he struck a deal to design couture and ready-to-wear collections for Balmain (p. 93). A decade later he resigned from the position to focus exclusively on his own line. His clientele remained the same: 'My customer is the over-30-year-old professional woman who likes to work and likes a lot of money, or a woman who is married and has a rich husband.'

Opposite An exercise in seductive seaming: Evening dress in cobalt blue with contrasting black triangular waist insert worn by Brooke Shields. 1983.

Oscar de la Renta

Above A political ambassador and de la Renta fan, Hillary Clinton wears a flesh-coloured, full-length evening dress overlaid with silver embellishment to the 1997 Presidential Inauguration.

Opposite Evening theatricality with shades of Catherine the Great: an extravagant de la Renta haute couture creation for Pierre Balmain, the toque trimmed in sable.

1920

1930

1932 Born Oscar Aristides Ortiz Renta Fiallo in Santo Domingo, Dominican Republic

1940

1951 Relocates to Madrid to study art at the Academy of San Fernando

1957 Works for Dior and Lanvin while on holiday in Paris

1960

1963 Debuts at Elizabeth Arden, New York

1965 Launches his own line; wins the Coty award

1970 Introduces menswear

1973 Elected to Coty Hall of Fame

1976 Miss O line launched

1980

1986 Becomes President of the CFDA

1990

1992 Secures a deal to design both ready to wear and couture collections for Balmain

1998 Hillary Clinton – the first First Lady to appear on the cover of Vogue – wears a dress by him

2000 Wins CFDA's Womenswear Design of the Year award

2010

2014 Dies in Connecticut, USA

'You are only as good as
the women you dress.'

Halston

1932–1990

UNITED STATES

With an identity that was inseparable from the legendary Studio 54 nightclub he frequented, Halston's profile was on a par with the celebrities he dressed. Preferring to eliminate any zips, buttons and superfluous fastenings, Halston made dresses to slide over the head and glide over the body. Applauded by his peers, Halston later explained: 'I cleaned up American fashion at a particular point in time. I was just getting rid of all the extra details that didn't work.' Fashion designer Bill Blass said: 'His clothes were American simplicity incarnate.'

Roy Halston Frowick was born in Des Moines, Iowa, but grew up in Indiana. As a student, he started making hats and charmed the hairdresser at Chicago's Ambassador Hotel into displaying his creations. A full-page feature in the *Chicago Daily News* meant he was soon making hats for celebrities including Deborah Kerr, Hedda Hopper and Kim Novak. At the age of 25, in 1957, he relocated to New York and secured a position with milliner Lilly Daché before becoming head milliner at the department store Bergdorf Goodman. 'Bergdorf's exposed me to the very best,' remembered Halston. 'I knew Balenciaga, I've stayed with Hubert de Givenchy. I met Coco Chanel. I saw Yves Saint Laurent's first collection.' While at Bergdorf's, he made the most famous pillbox hat in history, worn by Jacqueline Kennedy at President Kennedy's inauguration in 1961. In 1966, the first Halston boutique opened at Bergdorf Goodman. Opening Halston Ltd on Madison Avenue in 1968 with the backing of a Texan socialite, he stated: 'I fully intend to go into every aspect of fashion possible.'

His line initially included scarves, furs, shoes, belts, hats, jewellery and wigs. Later it extended to luggage, cosmetics, perfume, carpets and handbags. By the end of the 1970s, Halston had a total of 30 licensing deals. Fifty thousand women bought the Halston Ultrasuede shirtwaist dress.

In January 1978 Halston had achieved superstar status. He left his salon on East 68th Street and relocated his entire operation to a spectacular modernist, mirror-filled studio at Olympic Tower, taking the twenty-first floor above Fifth Avenue, with panoramic views of Manhattan and carpet woven with double Hs. The shows were described by close friend Andy Warhol as 'the art form of the seventies'. Halston's front row mixed celebrities, the Studio 54 set and New York socialites. Five years later Halston Enterprises was worth $150 million including $40 million in cosmetics.

Yet by the summer of 1984 the business had spiralled out of control. Revlon bought the Halston name in 1986, and Halston was no longer the president of his own company. The designer who once described his work as 'editing the mood of what was happening' spent the rest of his life outside the industry.

Opposite Devoid of any decoration or unnecessary detailing, the key to this example of elegant understatement is expert cutting and continuous colour.

Above Proving his talent was not confined to producing show-stopping eveningwear, Halston sits with models showing his dexterity for daywear. 1972.

Opposite top One of Halston's most loyal clients, Liza Minnelli, at their mutual hangout New York's Studio 54, 1979.

Opposite bottom Bianca Jagger, the perfect high-profile advertisement for the Halston look, wearing a jersey dress with a cowl neckline generous enough to drape over the head.

Halston

Born Roy Halston Frowick in Des Moines, Iowa, USA

Graduates from Bosse High School, Evansville, Indiana

Studies at the School of the Art Institute of Chicago while working as a window dresser

Opens first shop 'the Boulevard Salon' in the Ambassador Hotel, Chicago', then moves to New York

Jacqueline Kennedy wears hat design by Halston for her husband's presi... inauguration

1910   1920   1930 **1932**   1940   **'50** **'52**   **1957**   19 **1961**

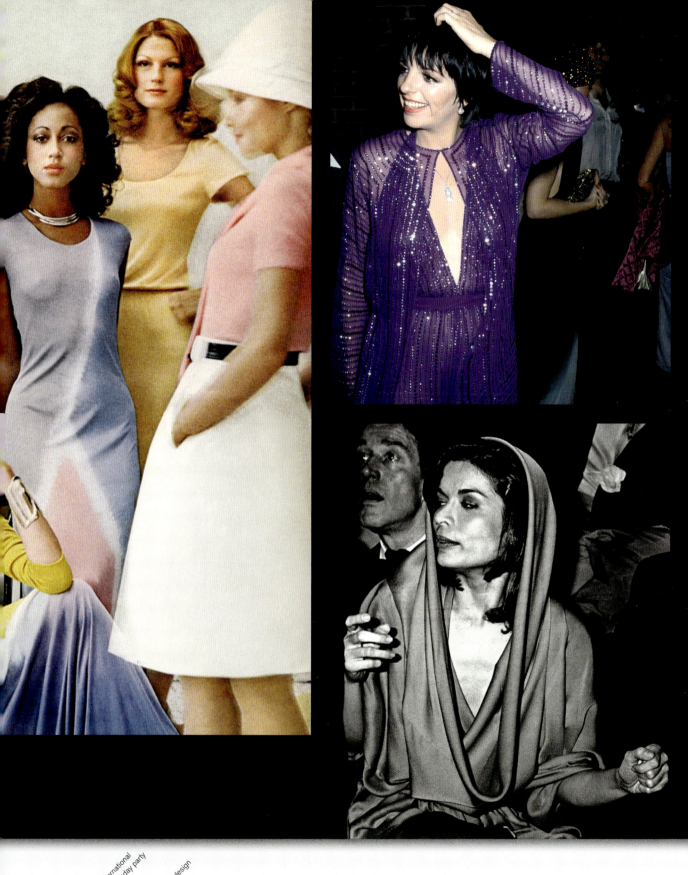

   1980 1986 1990 2000 2010

'I know what women want. They want to be beautiful.'

Valentino Garavani

b. 1932

ITALY

The Italian tastemaker whose lifestyle and collections embody the world of aspirational luxury summarized his talents in a sentence: 'There are only three things I can do – make a dress, decorate a house, and entertain people.' The Valentino empire, which embraced femininity and epitomized glamour, was founded in his favourite decade – the 1960s – a period he described as 'amazing but not too exaggerated'. As the 'new darling of the eminently fashionable', from the outset Valentino based his signature style on a single principle where elegance reigned supreme and no expense was spared in executing his ideas. The Roman couturier, whose fans included actresses Gina Lollobrigida, Sophia Loren, Audrey Hepburn and Elizabeth Taylor, built a reputation for dressing the world's most captivating beauties.

Born near Milan in the north of Italy, Valentino became interested in fashion when he watched movie stars Rita Hayworth and Gene Tierney at his local cinema. On leaving high school, he started to study fashion design and French in Milan, but at the age of 17 he departed for Paris, undertaking training at the École de la Chambre Syndicale de la Couture Parisienne and winning an International Wool Secretariat award. Securing a position at Jean Dessès, he assisted the couturier for five years before working for Guy Laroche.

On returning to Italy in 1959, Valentino opened his first couture studio. A fortuitous meeting with Giancarlo Giammetti, a student studying architecture, provided the business acumen and financial advice that would support Valentino throughout his career. Following his international debut at the Pitti Palace in Florence, the 1960s were a period of expansion and excitement for Valentino: appearing in *Vogue*, dressing society doyennes, making clothes for film stars and increasing his ateliers. In 1968, Valentino's all-white spring presentation captured the attention of Jacqueline Kennedy, who wore one of his dresses to marry shipping magnate Aristotle Onassis that year. The global coverage made Valentino an international name, and new lines were introduced, including accessories, fur, ready-to-wear, menswear and interior goods. Valentino boutiques opened in Rome, New York and Tokyo. In 1978 he made his first foray into perfume.

Celebrating a quarter of a century in fashion, Valentino created the outfits for the Italian Olympic team in 1984. He then introduced a denim line one year later that became phenomenally successful. Valentino staged his final haute couture show in the Musée Rodin, Paris, in January 2008. The rapturous applause and standing ovation from clients, admirers and industry insiders was a fitting tribute to the designer who maintained impeccable standards for 50 years. The focus of many exhibitions throughout his glittering career, Valentino was honoured by the building of a virtual Valentino museum, supervised by Giammetti, which used 3D technology to capture 180 fashion shows and 5,000 dresses.

Opposite To mark Valentino's last haute couture show at the Rodin Museum, Paris, a signature red finale saw models wearing identical backless, bias-cut column dresses. 2008.

Valentino Garavani

1920

1930

1932 Born in Voghera, Italy

1940

1950 Moves to Paris; takes classes at the École de la Chambre Syndicale de la Couture Parisienne; wins International Wool Secretariat award

1959 Establishes his own couture studio in Rome's Via Condotti

1962 Breakthrough show at the Palazzo Pitti in Florence; Giancarlo Giammetti becomes his business partner

1967 Establishes headquarters on Via Gregoriana, Rome

1970 Announces the arrival of the midi skirt; his company expands into accessories, fur and menswear

1975 Debut of Valentino ready-to-wear

1980

1984 Creates outfits for the Italian team at the Olympics

1986 Presented with the Cavaliere di Gran Croce, Italy's highest honour

1990

1992 30-year retrospective arrives in New York

1996 Receives the Cavaliere del Lavoro, equivalent of an Italian knighthood

2000 Celebrates 40 years in fashion and is given a Lifetime Achievement Award by the Council of Fashion Designers in America

2007 Announces his retirement as a retrospective – 'Valentino in Rome: 45 Years of Style' – is staged at the Ara Pacis Museum, Rome

2010

Opposite A strapless, monochrome
striped dress worn by supermodel Linda
Evangelista, subtly scalloped at the
edge, is accompanied by decorative
cuffs and patterned swing jacket. 1991.

Above This all-white collection, launched
in 1968, an era of fluorescent colour and
psychedelic pattern, was a sensation
and won Valentino a Neiman Marcus
award.

'One must never just wear a
dress. One must inhabit it.'

Emanuel Ungaro

b. 1933

FRANCE

Emanuel Ungaro was defined by *Women's Wear Daily* as
'The master technician who makes women look and feel
sexy'. The Ungaro label is inseparable from exuberance,
flirtatiousness and floral print. With a penchant for polka
dots, ruffles, drapery and painterly pattern, Ungaro is
regarded as the romantic designer who always infused
his designs with an implied sexuality. One of his most
devoted clients, Princess Catherine Aga Khan, explained:
'He understands how women like to provoke. His clothes
make you feel like a real woman.' Ungaro himself agreed:
'It's my will to seduce, and theirs too. It takes two to tango.'

As a child in Aix-en-Provence, the son of Italian
political refugees, Ungaro's first toy was a Singer sewing
machine. His father Cosimo, a tailor, taught him to sew by
the time he was 6 years old, and as a teenager he was
working in the family workshop. At the age of 23 he moved
to Paris and, after a couple of years working with various
tailors, he became an assistant to Cristóbal Balenciaga
(p. 53). He started in the sewing room stitching linings
and later learned his couture skills from the master over
a six-year period. Balenciaga, said Ungaro, 'blended
comfort and animation exceptionally. He was the father
of modern couture.' After briefly working for André
Courrèges (p. 113), who had also been a colleague at
Balenciaga, Ungaro opened his own house in 1965.

Ungaro initially ignored traditional couture protocol
and refused to show evening dresses, saying: 'They are
not my style.' His first collection, comprising 17 looks,
echoed Courrèges, with Space Age dresses and short
skirts. Then, in 1970, Ungaro changed course, developing
a signature that he summed up as 'flowers, romance and

baroque decoration'. It was a collection aimed not at
ingénues but at the more assured, mature woman of 35
to 55. The initial reaction from the press to his mixed-up
prints was to make Ungaro feel that he had been 'shot
down in flames', but even in the face of being called a
'terrorist' he was stubborn. Within a few seasons his
dream-like dresses garnered praise and a high-profile
following, attracting such actresses as Jean Seberg,
Catherine Deneuve and Anouk Aimée, the latter also
featuring in his advertisements.

Already an accomplished tailor, and introducing
immaculately cut suits into his collections, Ungaro
ventured into the menswear market in 1973, applying the
same attention to line and form. Having spent 40 years
at the helm of his own couture house, Ungaro retired in
2005. 'I learnt to work like this from Balenciaga,' he said.
'He used to say you have to work like a sculptor. Our
profession is not an art. It's a craft.'

Opposite Contrasting collared floral silk
jacket and diagonally woven wool tweed
skirt, abbreviated to mid-thigh worn with
a necklace all by Ungaro. 1982.

Sketches showing intense colour, short skirts, draped turbans and jackets where the neckline plunges to expose the décolletage. 1986.

Emanuel Ungaro

1920

1930

1933 Born in Aix-en-Provence, France

1940

1948 Learns tailoring techniques throughout his childhood from his father

1950

1958 Having moved to Paris, assists Cristóbal Balenciaga

1960

1965 After working briefly with André Courrèges, he opens his own fashion house in Paris

1968 Creates his Pret à Porter collection 'Parallele' and opens flagship boutique at 2 Avenue Montaigne, Paris

1970

1973 First menswear collection, entitled 'Ungaro Uomo'

1980

1983 Launches Diva perfume; Anouk Aimée becomes the face of the brand

1990

1996 Sells majority stake of his business to Salvatore Ferragamo

2000

2002 Launches diffusion line 'Fuchsia' and sportswear line 'Fever'

2005 Retires and sells his label to internet entrepreneur Asim Abdullah for $84 million

2010

This *Vogue* image from January 1986
shows the supremely confident Ungaro's
clash of patterns and impromptu
accessorizing.

'To create something exceptional, your mindset must be relentlessly focused on the smallest detail.'

Giorgio Armani

b. 1934

ITALY

The antithesis of Italian excess, Giorgio Armani brought fluid tailoring, immaculate understatement and the softly refined shoulder to the fashion arena. His minimalist approach in a traditionally maximalist culture was a complete sea change. Quietly and precisely, he questioned the status quo. 'My work today is perceived as classic,' said Armani, 'but when I first started out it was a break from the norm. Since then I have contrived to reinvent myself. I don't change my style, but I allow it to evolve.'

Devoid of drama and catwalk antics, Armani collections are a systematic presentation of wearable, desirable pieces often suffused with a neutral colour palette and occasionally overlaid with subtle embellishment. Armani's ability to underplay rather than overstate is key to his designer identity.

The clues to Armani's clean – almost clinical – approach to design are evident in his initial choice of career. With a grounding in medicine, he went on to do national service in the Italian Army. On leaving, he entered the fashion industry initially as a display designer and stylist, progressing to menswear buyer for the department store chain La Rinascente. His first foray into design was at Nino Cerruti, where, for a decade, he focused on menswear. He left to pursue a freelance career, launching his own menswear collection in 1975.

Expensive and instantly recognizable, Armani became the label of choice during the 'designer decade' of the 1980s. 'He has created a unique style, one that you can recognize without the label', said Carla Fendi in 1981. The following year, Armani became only the second fashion designer (after Christian Dior, p. 73) to feature on the cover of *Time* magazine, with the coverline 'Giorgio's Gorgeous Style'. Its air of executive success and subliminal message of self-assurance made the

Armani wardrobe prominent around the most powerful boardroom tables and then, having featured memorably in the film *American Gigolo* (1980), it achieved cinematic credibility. Such was Armani's supremacy on the red carpet that the 1989 Oscars were dubbed the 'Armani Awards'. Perhaps the ultimate compliment to Armani's art form was paid by director Martin Scorsese when he made a documentary about the elusive designer called *Made in Milan* (1990). Armani was also the first designer to feature on the Rodeo Drive Walk of Style.

Armani has, in common with his contemporaries, extended his brand to embrace an associated lifestyle. Not only has he produced complementary products – bed linen, towels and accessories ranging from silk stoles to iPad holders – but Armani, like Missoni, has also ventured into hotels. In 2008, he opened his largest store on Milan's Via Manzoni, followed by the Armani Hotel Milano in 2011. According to *Forbes* magazine, Italy's most successful designer had a net worth of $7.2 billion in March 2012.

Opposite The definitive trousersuit. Shoulderline, fit and detail has been redrawn over the seasons, but it is still the epitome of boardroom luxury. 1987.

Above Actor Richard Gere's appearance in *American Gigolo*, starring a wardrobe of Armani menswear, established the Italian designer in Hollywood. 1980.

Opposite Anne Hathaway at the Oscars wearing an iridescent champagne-coloured, Swarovski crystal and mother-of-pearl paillette dress from the Armani Privé collection, 2009.

Giorgio Armani

1920

1930

1934 Born in Piacenza, Italy

1940

1950

1960

Starts working for Nino Cerruti

1970 First design studio established in Milan

1970

1973 Establishes Giorgio Armani S.p.A. and shows his first menswear collection

1975 Designs for the film *American Gigolo*

1980 First Emporio Armani billboard

1984 Armani boutiques open in London and Beverly Hills

1988

1990

1999 Armani produces Martin Scorsese's film *Il Mio Viaggio in Italia*

2000 Launches bespoke Hand Made to Measure menswear service

2006 Largest store opens on Milan's Via Manzoni

2008

2010

'It's very important to take risks.'

Mary Quant

b. 1934

UNITED KINGDOM

'The young were taking over… Suddenly London was the most provocative and influential city in the world,' commented Mary Quant on the cataclysmic change that took place in Britain's capital during the 1960s. Quant was at the centre of it. Together with her husband, Alexander Plunket Greene, whom she described as 'a prototype for Mick Jagger and Paul McCartney rolled into one', she was part of what fashion editor Diana Vreeland called the 'youthquake'. Quant's simple daisy emblem signified optimism, vitality and cheek in equal measure.

Despite a mother and father who had both graduated from university with first-class degrees, Quant failed to attain her diploma at Goldsmiths College but it was there where her enthusiasm for fashion was fired up and where she met Plunket Greene. When Plunket Greene inherited £5,000 in 1955 they decided to start a business, and opened a shop called Bazaar near the King's Road, with a restaurant called Alexander's underneath. Armed with a sewing machine, a pair of dressmaking scissors and lengths of fabric purchased from Harrods' haberdashery department, Quant started to 'make the clothes that did not exist'.

The Quant look was the polar opposite of the structured, wasp-waisted New Look – short skirts, bright colours, bold graphics, all attached to Quant's daisy symbol. 'I seem to have the mind of a vacuum cleaner,' observed Quant. 'The pieces all turn into something else and one design turns into another.' From the jumbled assortment that Quant described as 'bedlam – a complete gamble' came a boutique that took the fashion world by storm. After opening a second Bazaar in Knightsbridge in 1957, within three years Quant had set her sights on America, securing a deal with department store Henri Bendel and wowing *Women's Wear Daily*, which reported: 'These Britishers have a massive

onslaught of talent, charm and mint-new ideas.' Quant struck up a deal with American retail giant JC Penney and by 1963 the Mary Quant simple daisy emblem was etched in the consumer consciousness. The former Chelsea boutique had become a global brand.

'Retailers and marketing men and women are born not made,' said Quant on how she achieved her success, 'but practice makes them as sophisticated and manipulative as a croupier.' A new line called Ginger Group was assembled, and in 1965 Quant secured her place in fashion history when she named her abbreviated skirt after her favourite car, the Mini. Mary Quant makeup with quirky titles and signature packaging was phenomenally successful. She even developed a cosmetic range – shocking at the time – for men. Her skincare range came complete with a set of vitamin pills and became part of the Quant package alongside lingerie, sportswear, hosiery, shoes, perfume, furs and homeware. 'It's the clothes, the walk, the hat, the hair, the gesture that I look forward to seeing when first meeting people,' said Quant. 'But it's the first effect that is so compelling.'

Opposite With the signature daisy dotted on watering cans, this 1967 collection featured stripes, zips, lace-trimmed hotpants and shiny multi-coloured boots.

Above Quirky, bold and capturing the imagination of the young, the Quant advertising campaigns were some of the most successful of the 1960s.

Opposite top Sweeping away 1950s propriety, this show from 1966 combined an irrepressible youthful attitude with opaque tights and mini hemlines.

Opposite bottom Supermodel of the era Jean Shrimpton in a polka-dot summer dress, suitably edged with a fluted neck trim and cuffs. 1964.

Mary Quant

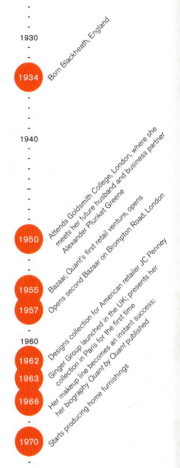

1920

1930

1934 Born Blackheath, England

1940

1950 Attends Goldsmith College, London, where she meets her future husband and business partner Alexander Plunket Greene

1955 Bazaar, Quant's first retail venture, opens

1957 Opens second Bazaar on Brompton Road, London

1960

1962 Designs collection for American retailer JC Penney

1963 Ginger Group launched in the UK; presents her collection in Paris for the first time

1966 Her makeup line becomes an instant success; her biography *Quant by Quant* published

1970 Starts producing home furnishings

1980

1988 Designs a Mini car featuring a daisy steering wheel

1990 Receives the British Fashion Council Hall of Fame Award

The Mary Quant Colour Shop opens

1994 Focuses on cosmetics and opens 50 boutiques specializing in makeup, mainly in Japan

1998

2000

2009 The new Quant miniskirt features on a Royal Mail stamp collection called 'British Design Classics'

'The best things I have ever
done have come from dreams.'

Karl Lagerfeld

b. 1938

GERMANY

Ageless, enigmatic and incredibly prolific, Karl Lagerfeld has the air of a French aristocrat and the wit of an impartial observer. 'I am a witness,' he said. 'An egotistical member of the audience who's never tired of watching the world from the dress circle.' In the same way that an Oscar-winning actor commands the screen, Lagerfeld has dominated the fashion scene for decades. With his signature sunglasses, high starched collar, fingerless gloves and ponytail, his outfit is his armour. 'I only know how to play one role,' he has declared. 'Me.' Lagerfeld's bons mots may be unpredictable, insightful and provocative, but his work is a constant. The designer who describes himself as 'a complete improvisation' has been at the helm of Chanel since 1983. He revolutionized the French house, which was floundering without its original founder (see Gabrielle Chanel, p. 41). 'For me work is cold, calm, organized,' he says. 'I hate hysteria.'

Lagerfeld was hired by Pierre Balmain (p. 93), then worked for Jean Patou and Chloé. His first fully fledged collection for Chloé was unveiled in October 1972 and he remained as head designer for more than a decade. Lagerfeld had been collaborating with the Italian fashion house Fendi since 1965, which specialized in furs.

When he was invited to reinvigorate Chanel, Lagerfeld recalled, 'Everybody said "Don't touch it. It's dead. It will never come back." But by then I thought it was a challenge.' Not only did he delight the fashion pundits with his reworking of Chanel, but the following

year, in 1984, he launched Karl Lagerfeld, his own label. During his tenure at Chanel he has introduced humour and youth, and has kept true to the Chanel signature, stating: 'My work is not to make the Chanel suit survive, but make it live.'

Lagerfeld varies his focus between being a designer, artist, writer, illustrator, photographer and even weight-loss guru. In 2001 he reinvented himself, losing more than 40 kg (90 lb) in order to wear slimline suits. 'I suddenly wanted to dress differently, to wear clothes designed by Hedi Slimane [p. 293],' he said. 'Fashion is the healthiest motivation for losing weight.' He entered the high street in 2004 by collaborating with H&M. A documentary entitled *Lagerfeld Confidential*, which took three years to film, was then released in 2007, giving a fascinating insight into Lagerfeld's personality, private life and working practices. 'I don't want to be real in other people's lives,' he said on celluloid. 'I want to be an apparition.'

Opposite Lagerfeld forged his reputation designing under the Chloé label, as here with a full-skirted silk dress using contrasting colourways. 1974.

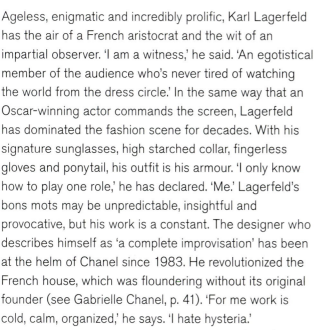

Karl Lagerfeld

Born in Hamburg, Germany

Having moved to Paris, Lagerfeld wins the Coat Category of the International Wool Secretariat Design Competition and becomes assistant to Pierre Balmain

Designs for Jean Patou, producing two couture collections per year

1910   1920   1930   **1938** 1940   1950   **1954** **1958** 960

Above Lagerfeld's debut collection for Chanel, 1983. 'I play with the elements like a musician plays with notes', he said.

Left Never afraid to push the boundaries, experiment and re-invent, Lagerfeld pairs traditional Chanel tweed with sheer and denim. 1991.

Opposite Often employing English muses to add edginess, Lagerfeld included Florence Welch performing 'What the Water Gave Me' from a giant seashell at Chanel's 2012 show.

Appointed Head Designer at Chloé

First full collection for Chloé

Presents first couture collection for Chanel

Starts Karl Lagerfeld label

Illustrates version of classic children's book, *The Emperor's New Clothes*

Collaborates with H&M

Lagerfeld Confidential film released

Presented with the Gordon Parks Foundation Award for his work as a designer, photographer and filmmaker

1966 · 1970 · 1972 · · · · 1980 · '83 '84 · · · · 1990 · 1992 · · · · 2000 · · · 2004 2007 · 201 2011 · · ·

'My design signature is constantly being shaped by new experiences.'

Barbara Hulanicki

b. 1936

POLAND

'The classic Biba dolly… was very pretty and young. She had an upturned nose, rosy cheeks and a skinny body and long asparagus legs… Her head was perched on a long, swanlike neck… She looked sweet but was as hard as nails,' wrote Barbara Hulanicki in her autobiography *From A to Biba* (1983). An accomplished illustrator who became a retail supremo, Hulanicki created an alternative reality for the 1960s customer. Dark, decadent and reminiscent of a Hollywood silent-movie set, the former Derry & Toms department store on London's Kensington High Street attracted up to a million customers a week. The Biba emporium was not only a product of its time but the first to capitalize on the concept of nostalgia. 'She gave us high street, high fashion,' observed Twiggy. 'We didn't have it before.'

Warsaw-born Hulanicki studied at the Brighton School of Art and showed early promise when she won a London *Evening Standard* beachwear competition in 1955. She worked freelance as a fashion illustrator, her drawings appearing in publications including *Vogue*, *Tatler* and *Women's Wear Daily*. With a desire to make youthful clothes for the masses, she started a business with her husband, Stephen Fitz-Simon. Of her working relationship with her husband, Hulanicki said, 'He did the production and business and left the dreaming to me.' 'We've got to do mail order,' he told her. 'That's the future.' Struggling to survive, they were about to give up when, in May 1964, Hulanicki was asked by the *Daily Mirror* to design a Brigitte Bardot-esque dress in gingham. One size, one colour: they received 17,000 orders. Supported by a series of mail order catalogues, and with the brand's image underlined by the distinctive Art Nouveau Biba logo, Hulanicki opened the first store in September 1964. Located in Kensington, it was informal, fun, affordable and an instant success. 'The louder the music

played the faster the girls moved and more people appeared in the shop,' recalled Hulanicki. 'I had sold every dress by 11 am.'

What later became known as 'Big Biba' opened a decade later. As much a visitor attraction as a shopping experience, the seven-storey department store gave free rein to Hulanicki's imagination. Ingeniously designed and irresistibly arranged, each floor had its own ambience. Hulanicki's vision went beyond the art of dressing – everything from baked beans to dog food was given the Biba treatment. Yet the cornerstone of the store was clothing. 'In those days a girl earnt £9 a week. So £3 for the bedsit, £3 for her food and £3 for her Biba dress.'

Although it became a magnet for film and rock stars, the shop was short-lived – but Biba's memory lives on. Now residing in Miami, Florida, where she reinvented herself as an interior designer, Hulanicki is still in demand. 'America has a completely different mindset,' she says. 'The past has no meaning. It's very interesting.'

Opposite The original 1960s supermodel, Twiggy, was both a Biba customer and advertisement for the brand (here photographed in 1975). 'It wasn't like any other shop I had ever seen,' she said.

Below From Biba's 1969 mail order catalogue, a battle-dress jacket in cotton drill with starched collar and turnback cuffs paired with a box pleat skirt.

Opposite Twiggy lounging in the deco decadence of Biba's department store dressed in a black sequinned tubular dress, split to the thigh and paired with pink suede shoes. 1971.

Barbara Hulanicki

Born in Warsaw, Poland

Family relocates to England

Studies fashion illustration at Brighton School of Art

Wins Evening Standard competition for beachwear

Launches mail order bi... Biba's Postal Boutiq...

1910	1920	1930	**1936**	1940	**1948**	950	**'54 '55**	1960	**'63**

Founds first Biba shop in Kensington, London

Biba opens larger store

Biba closes, selling 75% of its shares

Hulanicki moves to Miami to pursue interior design career

Returns to the fashion business with Fitz Fitz shop in downtown New York

Biba brand is relaunched

Hulanicki awarded an OBE; 'Biba & Beyond' exhibition staged at Brighton Museum and Art Gallery

64 · · · 1970 · · '73 '75 · · · 1980 · · · 1987 · 1990 · · · 1996 · · 2000 · · · · 2006 · · 2010 2012 · · ·

'A good model can advance
fashion by ten years.'

Yves Saint Laurent

1936–2008

ALGERIA

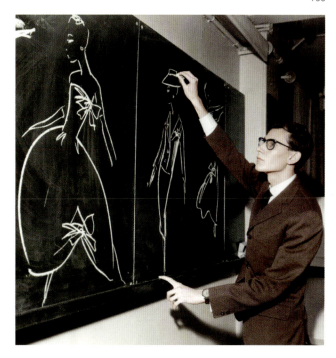

Famously fragile, incredibly prolific, and regarded as the tortured genius of quintessential French style, Yves Saint Laurent was a reclusive figure who dominated the couture scene for almost half a century. His elegant initials – YSL – were global shorthand for Parisian chic. Saint Laurent shunned the limelight, rarely gave interviews and preferred his seasonal collections to speak for themselves. His contradictory personality – definite in his taste, delicate in his constitution – were the unlikely traits of a couturier who simply called himself a 'crazy mixed-up man'.

Saint Laurent arrived in Paris from Oran, Algeria, in 1953. After winning an International Wool Secretariat competition he began his career in the illustrious company of Christian Dior (p. 73). At 21 years old, after the premature death of Dior, Saint Laurent was thrust into the spotlight as his unexpected successor. *Le Figaro* summed up the sentiments of a nation with its headline: 'Saint Laurent Has Saved France.'

Saint Laurent founded his own house in 1962. From the start, he was an unlikely maverick – on the surface the embodiment of the compliant couturier, but inside passionately committed to straddling the worlds of escapist couture and accessible ready-to-wear. His design handwriting blended masculine and feminine, dovetailing strict tailoring with flirtatious detail, pristine seam lines with flamboyant silhouettes. His most revolutionary reinvention – and the most internationally successful – was his womanly take on a man's tuxedo in 1966, christened 'Le Smoking'. He catered equally for women poised at the epicentre of high society and women who preferred the elegant end of street fashion. As his lifelong friend and long-term muse Catherine

Deneuve was to comment, 'Saint Laurent designs for women who lead double lives'.

From the 1960s, Saint Laurent's favourite artistic influences – Mondrian, Cocteau, Braque, Van Gogh and Picasso – appeared in a series of iconic fusions of fashion and fine art. In 1982 he declared: 'I am no longer concerned with sensation and innovation but the perfection of my style.' Diana Vreeland, a lifelong Saint Laurent fan, called him 'the master of the streets of the world'. Of the 1992 retrospective, the *New York Times* paid the highest compliment to Saint Laurent's legacy: 'What was wondrous about these clothes, besides their breathtaking beauty, was that nothing looked dated.'

Saint Laurent formally announced his retirement in 2002. His final couture collection was staged at the Centre Pompidou in Paris – a spectacular presentation of past and present – to an audience of more than 2,000 devotees. Jean Paul Gaultier (p. 249) said of his retirement: 'It is the departure of a myth. It is Garbo who is leaving.'

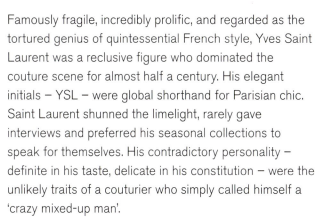

Opposite Yves Saint Laurent's muse, model and actress Catherine Deneuve, wears a strictly tailored double-breasted coat with leg-o'-mutton sleeves, 1970.

Opposite A year after his revolutionary 'Le Smoking' tuxedo, Saint Laurent presents his most androgynous statement in this outfit, elegantly echoing the composition of a man's pinstripe suit. Note the feminine sandal. 1967.

Below This modified geometric shift was directly inspired by Mondrian and made in wool jersey. It featured on the cover of French *Vogue* in September 1965.

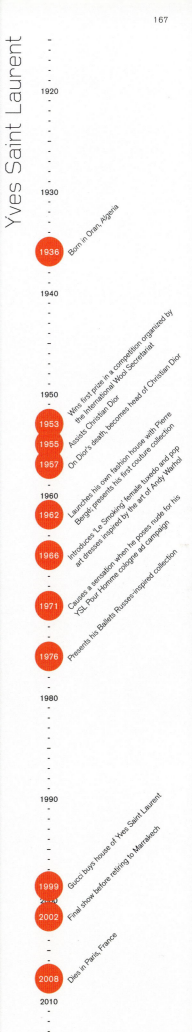

Yves Saint Laurent

1920

1930

1936 Born in Oran, Algeria

1940

1950

1953 Wins first prize in a competition organized by the International Wool Secretariat
Assists Christian Dior

1955 On Dior's death, becomes head of Christian Dior

1957 Launches his own fashion house with Pierre Bergé; presents his first couture collection

1960

1962 Introduces 'Le Smoking' female tuxedo and pop art dresses inspired by the art of Andy Warhol

1966 Causes a sensation when he poses nude for his YSL Pour Homme cologne ad campaign

1971 Presents his Ballets Russes-inspired collection

1976

1980

1990

1999 Gucci buys house of Yves Saint Laurent

2002 Final show before retiring to Marrakech

2008 Dies in Paris, France

2010

'From the beginning, I thought about the body in movement.'

Issey Miyake

b. 1938

JAPAN

'Issey Miyake makes it possible for everyone to look gorgeous in a sack – what am I saying? Everyone looks extraordinary, like a moving monument,' observed actress Tilda Swinton, wearing one of Miyake's outfits for the *Sunday Times*. Miyake's customers have ranged from American jazz impresario Miles Davis to British thespian Maggie Smith. *Time* magazine called him 'an adamant modernist, a determined internationalist'. The fashion industry views him as an experimentalist who rewrote the rulebook on fashion.

In his first presentation in 1963, entitled 'Poems of Cloth and Stone', a model stripped off pieces of cloth until she stood naked before the audience. Despite his avant-garde approach, Miyake cites the kimono and the British raincoat as two of his all-time favourite garments. He believes ease transcends all kinds of clothes – from traditional tailoring to experimental cutting. 'You put it on and it is as though you have always worn it,' he says. 'My clothes are born out of the movements of my hands and body. I want the body of the wearer, her individuality, to make the shape of the clothes.'

Miyake was born in Hiroshima and was 7 years old when the atomic bomb was dropped. Most of his family were lost, his mother, a schoolteacher, dying later of radiation exposure. 'I tried never to be defined by my past,' he told the *New York Times* in 2009. 'I did not want to be labeled "the designer who survived the atomic bomb".' At the age of 26, Miyake left Tama Art University in Tokyo with a degree in graphic design. Describing fashion as 'a creative format that is modern and optimistic', he trained in Paris with Guy Laroche and Givenchy (p. 117) before learning the art of merchandising in New York. In 1970 Miyake returned to Tokyo to open his design studio and the following year

presented his first Spring/Summer collection in New York. He had already decided Paris couture was not for him: 'So beautiful, so static. Stuck, the society also.'

With the launch of 'Pleats Please' in 1993, the Miyake brand extended its appeal beyond aficionados to what Miyake called 'ordinary people'. 'I know some people are frightened of my clothes,' he had said in 1990, 'but at least that means they are responding, expressing emotion. If people do not have that emotion, then I know that it's not worked.'

He worked continually on the concept of 'A piece of cloth', called A-POC, starting in 1997 as a project led by Miyake and engineering designer Dai Fujiwara. During the 1980s, Miyake called his experimental creations 'Bodyworks'. He also collaborated with distinguished photographer Irving Penn. For Miyake, the fabric is fundamental – not only as the foundation of the design but as the barometer of the ebb and flow of the garment. 'Fabric is like the grain in wood; you can't go against it. Sometimes I like to close my eyes and let the fabric tell me what to do.'

Opposite Ardent Miyake fan Grace Jones wears a typically avant-garde, organic and striking pleated creation. 1994.

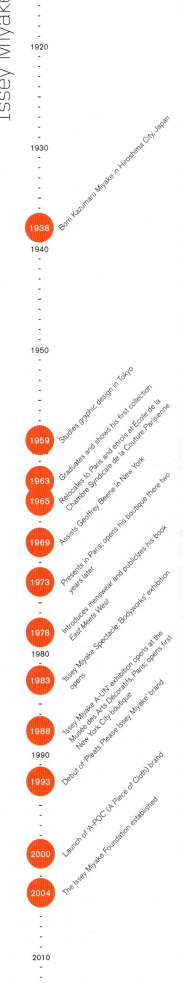

1920

1930

1938 Born Kazumaru Miyake in Hiroshima City, Japan

1940

1950

1959 Studies graphic design in Tokyo

Graduates and shows his first collection

1963 Relocates to Paris and enrols at École de la Chambre Syndicale de la Couture Parisienne

1965 Assists Geoffrey Beene in New York

1969 Presents in Paris; opens his boutique there two years later

1973 Introduces menswear and publicizes his book *East Meets West*

1978 'Issey Miyake Spectacle: Bodyworks' exhibition opens

1980

1983 'Issey Miyake A-UN' exhibition opens at the Musée des Arts Décoratifs, Paris; opens first New York City boutique

1988 Debut of 'Pleats Please Issey Miyake' brand

1990

1993 Launch of 'A-POC' (A Piece of Cloth) brand

2000 The Issey Miyake Foundation established

2004

2010

Opposite Miyake, together with engineering designer Fujiwara, developed the ultimate example of customized clothing entitled 'A-POC' (A Piece Of Cloth). The brand debuted in Paris in 1997, launching three years later.

Above Movable, collapsible synthetic pleated dresses are a recurring Miyake signature. These 'Minaret' pleats are from Spring/Summer 1995.

'Fashion comes from outside the mainstream. That is what makes fashion so interesting.'

Kenzo Takada

b. 1939

JAPAN

Capturing the spirit of the early 1970s, Kenzo Takada perfectly crystallized the mood of the moment, combining kaleidoscopic colours and cultural diversity with an Eastern sensibility. 'His designs were very clever, completely cutting edge at the time,' recalled the photographer and former Kenzo model Ellen von Unwerth. Kenzo's ability to clash prints, mix textures and invigorate his collections with a vibrant colour palette earned him the title 'the Little Prince of Fashion'. It was not unusual to see Peruvian wraps, florals, paisleys and woolly pompoms appear in a single outfit. Pre-empting the United Colors of Benetton advertising campaigns by a decade, Kenzo promoted his vision of multicultural unity initially under the ironic title 'Jungle Jap' and later under his own name. 'When I'm in Tokyo, I feel French,' he told the New York Times in 1983. 'When I'm in Paris, Japanese.'

Kenzo studied literature at Kobe University but left to take up fashion at Bunka Gakuen University in Tokyo. He won a magazine design competition, and in 1964 satisfied his nomadic tendencies by buying a one-way ticket to Europe for a six-week tour. Showing his sketches to the fashion houses in Paris, he was hired to work freelance for Pierre Cardin (p. 105). His first presentation took place in a vacant boutique in Galerie Vivienne. 'I wanted to call it Jungle Something. Jungle Jap sounded good – it had humour – so I painted that on the window,' he said. 'I wanted to make dresses that ordinary women could afford. In those days it was easy to take risks.'

Kenzo became known for ethnic irreverence, taking the basis of a kimono and translating it into an unexpected fabric. He dismissed the conventions of traditional tailoring and seasonal coloration. The basis for his fashion was fantasy: 'For those wearing my clothes, it is like stepping out of ordinary life and into a dream.' His collections during the 1970s took inspiration from around the globe – Austrian dirndls, Portuguese purses, African boubous, Chinese pyjamas, English raincoats. Kenzo was at the forefront of the artisan era, a look the Times called 'mixed-up dressing', prompting them to hail his influence as 'second only to Saint Laurent'.

His final show, in Paris in October 1999, prompted Vogue to report on the 'runway appearances by his friends Pat Cleveland and model Katoucha Niane and a cameo by Shanga, a 40-year-old Indian elephant'.

Quintessential Kenzo from 1973 featured clashing prints, contradictory colourways and a playful notion of fashion.

Left Bohemian patterns, bold colour, ethnic accessories and a conventional waistcoat work brilliantly together. 2014.

Opposite A modern interpretation of the original kimono with broad edging and reworked proportions. 1996.

Kenzo Takada

Born in Himeji, Japan

Enrols as one of the first male students at Bunka Gakuen Fashion School, Tokyo

Freelances for Pierre Cardin

Establishes his own store in Galerie Vivienne; stages first show at his boutique 'Jungle Jap'

| | 1920 | | 1930 | | **1939** 0 | | 1950 | | **1957** 1960 | | **1965** | | **1970** | |

Launches menswear collection; Kenzo boutique
opens in Manhattan
Kenzo Jeans and Kenzo Jungle diffusion lines
are launched.

LVMH purchases Kenzo's fashion and
perfume business

Exhibition at Musée de la Mode, Marseille;
announces his retirement and shows final
Paris collection

Humberto Leon and Carol Lim named as
Creative Directors of Kenzo

1980   **1983** **1986**   1990   **1993**   **1999** 0   201**2011**

'Sportswear is about living, and that's where America has made its mark.'

Ralph Lauren

b. 1939

UNITED STATES

A former tie salesman who reigns supreme in the fine art of fashion marketing, Ralph Lauren once said, 'I don't design clothes, I design dreams'. His storytelling qualities are legendary, his ability to conjure aspirational images unrivalled and his attention to detail – particularly in creating retail environments with an aristocratic ambience – is second to none. 'There has been a remarkable consistency to his imagination,' said *Vogue* in 1992, as he celebrated 25 years in the business. Almost a quarter of a century later, the same sentiment applies.

With a foundation in the cut and thrust of retail, Lauren has no formal training in fashion design, but something just as valuable: an inherent understanding of the customer. His clothes are essentially classic, unobtrusive, perennially wearable. Sold in elegant surroundings, the Ralph Lauren collection seamlessly echoes the images of bygone eras. He interweaves style with narrative, always imbuing his collections with an enviable lifestyle. He moves deftly between eras and movie-set scenarios, with recurring themes being played out season after season: the prairie pioneer, the polo player, the English aristocrat, the Ivy League student. Adamant that his design signature is not retrospective, he says: 'What I stand for is quality and timelessness. The clothes are not about nostalgia, not about yesterday; they're about forever.'

Born Ralph Lifshitz in the Bronx to a family of Belarusian immigrants, he toyed with the idea of being an artist or a basketball player. He settled on a career in selling, joining Allied Stores at the age of 19 as an assistant buyer and formed his own company, Polo Fashions Inc., a decade later. 'There were no rules for me,' he has said. 'I made them up as I went along.' Originally focusing on menswear, he cites Fred Astaire, Cary Grant and the Duke of Windsor as his all-time sartorial heroes.

Believing he was his own best advertisement, from 1974 Lauren starred in his own publicity shots, becoming the face of the brand. In April 1986, he opened his flagship store on Madison Avenue in New York – a palatial shop that *Women's Wear Daily* described as 'an ode to the English gentry' and the journal's publisher John Fairchild applauded as 'the best boutique in America – and probably the world'.

With a fashion philosophy where lifestyle is the lifeblood of the business, today the Ralph Lauren label can be found on luggage, spectacles, underwear, sportswear, sheets, towels and tableware. In 2013 the billionaire Lauren, already established as a philanthropist, pledged millions to modernize the École nationale supérieure des Beaux-Arts in Paris.

Opposite Relaxed, imbued with ease, and essentially all-American, the Ralph Lauren label is a global phenomenon.

Opposite top The androgynous wardrobe for Diane Keaton's kooky character in Woody Allen's *Annie Hall* in 1977 was one of the seminal looks of the decade.

Opposite bottom Robert Redford, playing a leading role in *The Great Gatsby* (1974) was immaculately dressed by Ralph Lauren.

Above A perennial theme in the collections is the Navajo Indian dress, not only in knitwear and textiles but also accessories. 1981.

Ralph Lauren

1920

1930

1939 Born Ralph Lifshitz in the Bronx, New York, USA

1950

1959 Studies business for two years at Baruch College in New York

1960

1964 After leaving the US Army Reserve, works as a tie salesman at Brooks Brothers and Beau Brummell

1968 Starts designing menswear under the Polo Ralph Lauren label before opening a boutique within Bloomingdales Department store

1970

1974 Designs costumes for male cast of *The Great Gatsby*

1977 Designs costumes for Diane Keaton in *Annie Hall*

1980

1983 Launches Ralph Lauren Home collection and shows his Safari collection

1986 Re-opens flagship store on Manhattan's Madison Avenue

1990

1992 Receives a Lifetime Achievement Award from the CFDA

1996 Launches Polo Jeans collection

1999 Opens flagship store on London's Bond Street

2000

2006 Becomes the first official designer of outfits for Wimbledon tennis tournament

2011 His car collection is exhibited at the Musée des Arts Décoratifs in Paris

'Fashion will last forever.
It will exist always.'

Azzedine Alaïa

b. 1940

TUNISIA

Advocating a sinuous silhouette in an era of flamboyance, Azzedine Alaïa was hailed 'the King of Cling'. His suggestion in the early 1980s that clothes should closely follow the contours of a woman's figure was a complete contradiction of mainstream fashion. Since the debut of his first ready-to-wear collection in 1980, Alaïa has reigned supreme in the art of body-conscious structure. His particular vision of femininity – powerful, fearless, unashamedly sexy – is displayed to its best advantage on Amazonian models with elongated limbs.

Away from the catwalk, the Alaïa label has engendered a cult-like following. He has designed one-off pieces for some supremely stylish individuals, including a voluminous coat for Greta Garbo and a French tricolour gown for Jessye Norman. Few designers in the history of fashion have his rapport with the female anatomy. Fittingly, Alaïa calls himself a *bâtisseur*, or master builder, rather than a fashion designer.

Alaïa's materials of choice are supple, luxurious, invariably imbued with elastication – synthetic knit, rayon jersey, leather. His preferred method of decoration is not superfluous embroidery or intricate beadwork but simple, precisely positioned repeat patterns, often laser-cut into leather. Obsessed with evolution rather than revolution, refinement rather than compromise, Alaïa has always resolutely refused to play the fashion game. He is not interested in making seasonal statements, always presenting his collections out of sync with the fashion calendar. Bizarrely for one who built his reputation on body-consciousness, his style icon – the late Queen Elizabeth the Queen Mother – was perennially swathed in chiffon, in colours resembling a sugar-coated confection.

A Tunisian maverick, at the age of 18 Alaïa spent five days at Dior (p. 73) before being dismissed. This was followed by two seasons at Guy Laroche and a brief spell at Thierry Mugler (p. 229). He established his first atelier in the late 1970s. Decades later, when John Galliano (p. 273) was ejected from Dior, Alaïa was offered the position. He refused. Although fiercely independent, Alaïa entered into a business arrangement with Prada (p. 237) in 2000. Ostensibly to expand the brand, the prime motivation according to Alaïa was not financial, but rather to secure the future of his archive. Alaïa's personal collection – one of the most comprehensive in the world – includes examples of couture perfection from Adrian, Charles James (p. 81) and Vionnet (p. 29).

Officially recognized as a couturier in 2011 by the Chambre Syndicale de la Haute Couture, Alaïa has dressed Michelle Obama, Carine Roitfeld, Carla Bruni and Lady Gaga, and his style is as relevant now as it was in the 1980s. Naomi Campbell, who has been modelling for Alaïa since she was 16 years old, describes his rarefied technique as 'almost magical. No other dress can make a woman look and feel as good.'

Opposite Always with an exacting eye for detail, Alaïa designed timeless and distinctive outfits like this tailored leather bestseller. 1990.

A seductive alternative to the 1980s
power suit, Alaïa's elasticated dressing
was a revelation. 1986.

Azzedine Alaïa

1920

1930

1940 — Born in Tunis, Tunisia

1950

1954 — Studies sculpture at École des Beaux-Arts, Paris

1960

1970

1981 — Shows his first collection having opened an atelier on Paris's Left Bank in the late 1970s

1988 — Opens boutique on Mercer Street, Manhattan

1990

1992 — Opens Paris store

2000 — Sells business to Prada group and establishes Alaïa Foundation

2007 — Buys back business and sells it to Richemont Group

2010

2013 — Retrospective at Paris's Musée Galliera and Musée d'Art

'I have an in-built clock that always reacts against anything orthodox.'

Vivienne Westwood

b. 1941

UNITED KINGDOM

Dame Vivienne Westwood is the ultimate conundrum. Equal parts visionary and historian, she lives in private without the accoutrements of the modern world – mobile phone, television, Internet access – but is known internationally as the embodiment of forward thinking. A revolutionary without equal, she has unleashed her fertile imagination on the fashion world for more than 40 years.

A former primary-school teacher, Westwood hails from the countryside of Derbyshire and moved to London as a teenager when her parents relocated to the metropolis. She married airline steward Derek Westwood at the age of 21, and a year later her first son was born. It was a fateful meeting in 1965 with situationist art student Malcolm McLaren – a friend of her brother Gordon's – that was to transform Westwood from conventional housewife to charismatic pioneer whose creative drive would change the British sartorial landscape forever. Together she and McLaren launched a series of radical retail experiences on London's King's Road – in the form of a shop known variously as Let It Rock, Too Fast To Live, Too Young to Die, Sex, and Seditionaries. In 1976, deploying the Sex Pistols as their musical mannequins, Westwood and McLaren created the most potent street style of the twentieth century: punk.

Often decades ahead of her time, Westwood has, since her first formal collection in 1981, entitled 'Pirate', continued to fascinate the fashion pundits and stun her detractors. Her subsequent early collections – 'Buffalo Girls', 'Witches', 'Punkature', 'Hypnos', 'Harris Tweed', 'Mini Crini', 'Pagan' – were groundbreaking not only in their pattern-cutting technique but in the thought processes behind them. Gathering eclectic sources of inspiration – ranging from Greek mythology to Dior's New Look – she redefined the silhouette, reintroduced platform shoes and reinvigorated global interest in traditional British cloth. Believing that in English dressing 'every fabric has an emotional charge', she has continually rewritten the rules on tailoring.

From the early 1990s she embraced elegance as her new watchword. In 1994 *Vogue* declared her 'probably England's greatest fashion designer of this century'.

Opposite Extravagance personified, Linda Evangelista wears an asymmetrically cut 'Watteau' silk taffeta dress with train at the back and flamboyant bows at the front. Spring/Summer 1996.

Opposite Singer Chrissie Hinde, shop assistant Jordan and Westwood make a subversive line up in her shop Sex on London's Kings Road.

Above A typically cavalier look which takes key historic detail interpreted into a contemporary outfit. 1995.

Below Westwood made her debut as a fully-fledged fashion designer with the 'Pirate' collection of A/W 1981.

1920

1930

1941 Born in Tintwistle, England

1950

1960

1971 Opens Let it Rock boutique with Malcolm McLaren subsequently renamed Too Fast To Live, Too Young To Die (1972), Sex (1974) Seditionaries (1977), and World's End (1980)

Presents first collection, 'Pirate'

1980 First Paris show
1982

1990

Receives OBE

1992 'Anglomania' collection launched
1993

2000

Made Dame Vivienne Westwood

2006 Launches Active Resistance to Propaganda
2007 manifesto

2010

'Beautiful or stylish is a personal feeling. I don't have a definition of beauty.'

Rei Kawakubo

b. 1942

JAPAN

Austere, definite, esoteric, Rei Kawakubo has been questioning the status quo since the 1970s. 'Not what has been seen before. Not what has been repeated. Instead, new discoveries that look towards the future, that are liberated and lively. This is Comme des Garçons,' read the directive for Kawakubo's 1997 collection. The statement summed up the company philosophy. Together with Yohji Yamamoto (p. 209), Kawakubo made fashion history in 1981 when she was invited to show at the Paris collections. Though her look was dubbed 'Hiroshima chic' and the 'bag lady look' by fashion journalists, the interplay of radical cutting, off-centre seaming, experimental shaping and textural intervention blew any preconceived ideas away. Running parallel to Vivienne Westwood's ethos (p. 185), Rei Kawakubo's take on fashion was more alarming, less palatable. 'Oblique Chic,' wrote *Vogue*. 'Once you get the hang of it it is something marvellous.'

Rei Kawakubo originally had no intention of becoming a fashion designer, instead studying fine art at Tokyo's Keio University. It was while promoting acrylic fibres for a Japanese chemical company that she started to make her own clothes, and coined the name 'Comme des Garçons'. After freelancing, she officially launched the label in 1973 but was not exposed to an international audience until 1981.

Initially greeted with incomprehension, the Comme des Garçons label grew sufficiently to make Kawakubo a significant player in the fashion world. By the end of the 1980s, Comme des Garçons was turning over more than $100 million a year and had more than 300 outlets internationally. The brand had expanded extensively to include menswear, knitwear and linen for the bathroom and bedroom. Kawakubo diversified into furniture in 1987, producing a range that included spiral chairs in clear acrylic and chrome-plated steel. She viewed them as pieces of sculpture. In the same year, Kawakubo was given the ultimate accolade when she was included as part of a trio of revolutionary designers in a show called 'Three Women: Madeleine Vionnet, Claire McCardell and Rei Kawakubo' at the Fashion Institute of Technology in New York.

Kawakubo's 1996 'Dress Meets Body, Body Meets Dress' collection proved too extreme even for the fashion savvy and was unkindly christened the 'Quasimodo collection'. The padded inserts distorted the silhouette and became a focus of ridicule. Kawakubo remained unfazed. After the turn of the millennium she continued to expand her retail operations, launching a series of pop-up shops and an exclusive outlet in London's Dover Street. Reflecting on the furore of 1996, she told the *New Yorker* that she 'never intended to start a revolution'.

Opposite Entitled 'White Drama', this collection blended ceremonial and stately dress with a conceptual edge. Spring/Summer 2012.

Opposite This black ensemble was designed by Rei Kawakubo for Comme des Garçons in 1982. It consists of a hand-knitted jumper decorated with randomly placed holes, giving it a post-Punk era feel, and a skirt of padded cotton jersey.

Right and below The 'Body meets Dress. Dress meets Body' collection of Spring/Summer 1997 questioned preconceived ideas on fashion design. The bodily distortion created by avant-garde cutting and padding was an acquired taste that divided the critics.

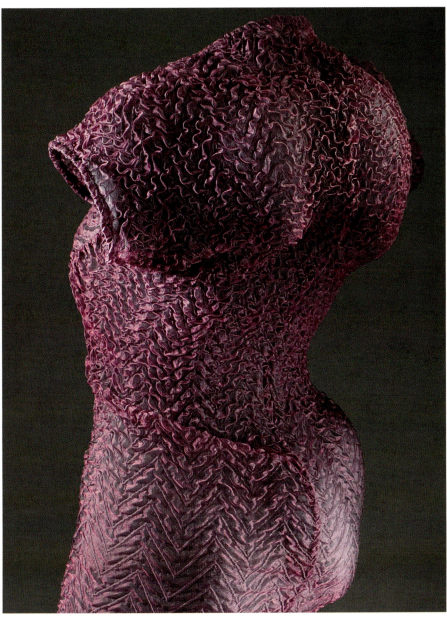

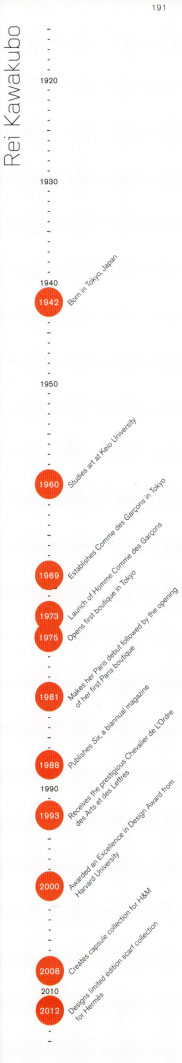

Rei Kawakubo

1920

1930

1940

1942 Born in Tokyo, Japan

1950

1960 Studies art at Keio University

1969 Establishes Comme des Garçons in Tokyo

1973 Launch of Homme Comme des Garçons

1975 Opens first boutique in Tokyo

1981 Makes her Paris debut followed by the opening of her first Paris boutique

1988 Publishes Six, a biannual magazine

1990

1993 Receives the prestigious Chevalier de L'Ordre des Arts et des Lettres

2000 Awarded an Excellence in Design Award from Harvard University

2008 Creates capsule collection for H&M

2010

2012 Designs limited edition scarf collection for Hermès

Calvin Klein Jeans

'I'm a sexual person, and that's reflected in my clothes and my advertisements.'

Calvin Klein

b. 1942

UNITED STATES

As synonymous with American understatement as he was with advertising campaigns, Calvin Klein captured the zeitgeist for two decades. His design signature – blending purist overtones with a sexual undercurrent – sparked a retail phenomenon that catapulted a boy from the Bronx to fashion superstardom. A fixture on the Studio 54 circuit and no stranger to controversy, throughout his career Klein trod the fine line between stylish provocateur and instigator of public outrage. In the 1990s he was accused of advocating 'heroin chic', but he had first caused a stir in 1980, when an adolescent Brooke Shields posing seductively in his skintight jeans on a TV advertisement asking, 'Do you want to know what comes between me and my Calvins? Nothing.' The combination of youth and sexual innuendo had the desired impact, not lessened by accusations of child pornography: 200,000 pairs sold in their first week.

Klein always looked beyond clothes to the bigger picture. 'I started my own in-house agency from the day I started my business,' he told New York's *Interview* magazine. He worked in the art department at *Women's Wear Daily* and apprenticed for coat maker Dan Millstein. In 1968, with a $10,000 loan from his best friend (and later business partner) Barry Schwartz and $2,000 of his own money, Klein established Calvin Klein Ltd.

Success came quickly. In its first season, the company grossed $500,000. The following year, one of Klein's coats was featured on the cover of *Vogue*. In 1973 he switched to sportswear and won two consecutive Coty awards. He made an initial, unsuccessful range of designer jeans in 1976, but by modifying the fit and shape he had secured a fifth of the market just three years later. Klein was interviewed by *Playboy*, introduced a fragrance called Obsession, and

transformed the men's underwear market by putting his name on the elasticated waistband. By the end of the 1980s, Klein had made changes in his personal life, marrying Kelly Rector, a former design assistant, and buying a new home on Long Island. In 1989 the company, whose income had escalated thanks to fragrance sales, was turning over $1.2 billion.

Cited as one of the 25 most influential Americans by *Time* magazine in 1996, Klein continued to create collections that combined elements of androgyny – a masculine jacket over a feminine dress – and maintained that his customer was someone who 'wants to feel like a woman without being treated as a fashion trophy'. In 1995 Klein launched CK One, his hugely successful unisex fragrance.

In 2003 Klein sold his business to the shirtmaker Phillips-Van Heusen for $430 million but stayed in the business. Three years later he walked away from the company he had founded. 'I've always been the kind of person who does all or nothing.'

Opposite An adolescent Brooke Shields became the public face and body of Klein's groundbreaking advertising campaigns. 1980. Photograph by Richard Avedon © The Richard Avedon Foundation.

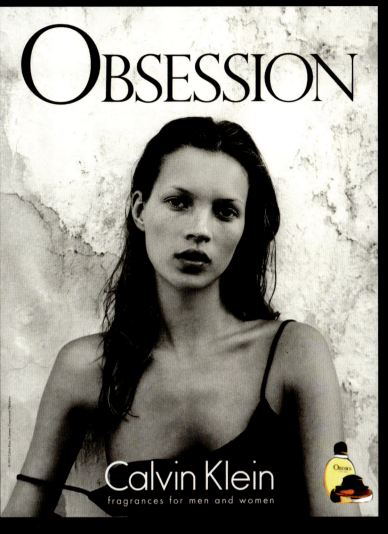

OBSESSION

Calvin Klein
fragrances for men and women

Opposite A purist, pared-down look. Autumn 2010.

Above A nineteen-year-old Kate Moss captured the essence of innocence and sexual attraction which the 'Obsession' fragrance wanted to convey. 1993.

Below This glistening strapless cocktail dress has discreet horizontal lines and a matching clutch bag. 1989.

Calvin Klein

1920

1930

1940

1942 Born in the Bronx, New York, USA

1950

1960

1962 Studies at FIT but leaves before graduation to work at garment manufacturer Dan Millstein

1967 Establishes Calvin Klein Ltd with Barry Schwartz; premieres the following year

1970

1973 Launches cosmetics line

1980

1982 Underwear for men launched; women's line launched the following year

1985 Launch of Obsession perfume with $17 million campaign, on which Bruce Weber, Richard Avedon and David Lynch are all employed to work

1990

1993 Debut of CK diffusion line followed by CK One, the first unisex eau de toilette

2000

2003 Calvin Klein Inc. sold to Phillips-Van Heusen Corp; Receives honorary doctorate from FIT, New York

2010

'I don't care how much anything costs, so long as it's beautiful.'

Ossie Clark

1942–1996

UNITED KINGDOM

'It's just something I have in my hands' – this was Ossie Clark's instinctive explanation of the incredible talent he had for pattern cutting. No one in the history of fashion, bar perhaps Balenciaga (p. 53), Vionnet (p. 29) or Madame Grès (p. 69), had Clark's aptitude for taking a length of fabric and turning it into an exquisite work of art. Clark's genius lay in his ability to infuse beautiful clothes with an inherent sensuality. He made dresses to dance in, relax in, move around in – they were never stiff or static. He was incapable of making untouchable entities to be admired from a distance. 'Comfort,' he once said. 'That's the most important thing.' His designs were elevated to another level by his creative partnership – unique in the fashion industry – with textile designer Celia Birtwell, whose painterly prints perfectly complemented Clark's undulating line. The pair epitomized the Swinging Sixties.

Raymond Clark was born into a large working-class family in Liverpool and was evacuated to Oswaldtwistle, Lancashire, during the war, from which he gained his nickname, Ossie. At secondary school Clark was introduced to the world of glamour via a schoolmaster who brought him glossy fashion magazines. After studying art and architecture in Manchester, Clark found his natural métier when he was granted a scholarship to London's Royal College of Art. In 1965, taught by the influential principal Janey Ironside, Clark graduated with an Op Art collection, a first-class honours degree and full-page coverage in *Vogue*. His portrait and one of his coats, modelled by Chrissie Shrimpton, were photographed by David Bailey and he was later dubbed 'the King of King's Road'.

Clark immediately established his own label, joining forces with retailer Alice Pollock, promoting and selling his collection from the Quorum boutique on London's King's Road. 'All sorts of people used to hang out there,' said model Patti Boyd. 'The building was a mecca for the young and the beautiful.'

At the core of Clark's success was the potent combination of romanticism and sexuality. He was amazingly versatile, as adept at handling snakeskin as he was at arranging reams of chiffon. With an attitude that was more rock star than fashion designer, Clark choreographed the concept of the fashion 'happening', where models danced animatedly and interacted with the audience. Ossie Clark shows at Chelsea Town Hall in 1970 and, particularly, at the Royal Court Theatre in 1971, have been cited as landmark fashion moments.

Out of sync with the mass market, Clark nevertheless adapted to mainstream fashion by producing a ready-to-wear line under the Radley label. 'I thought his garments were wonderful,' said Birtwell of his early creations. 'He was a real artist.'

Opposite A quintessential example of Birtwell's illustrative print and Clark's creative cutting coming together in sheer chiffon and matte silk. 1969.

Above Celia Birtwell's simplistic textile designs – floating daisy and candy flower – decorate a crepe Ossie Clark dress. 1970.

Opposite Commissioned to provide costumes for Mick Jagger, Clark created a series of velour jumpsuits sporadically decorated with sequins. 1973.

1920

1930

1940

1942 Born Raymond Clark in Liverpool, England

1950

1959 Meets Celia Birtwell in Manchester via mutual friend Mo McDermott

1962 Studies fashion design at the Royal College of Art

1965 Graduates with first class honours and features in British *Vogue*

1969 Mick Jagger wears Ossie Clark on tour; marries Birtwell

1970 Painted with his wife Celia by David Hockney in *Mr and Mrs Clark and Percy*

1975 Quorum boutique closes

1980

1983 Creates costumes for Sir Frederick Ashton's ballet *Vari Capricci*

1990

1996 Dies in London, England

2000

2010

'I am convinced you don't have to spend a fortune to look like a million.'

Jil Sander

b. 1943

GERMANY

Famously private and a perfectionist to her fingertips, Jil Sander brought minimalism to the fore in the 1990s. Her brand of simplicity, which merged clean lines with understated colours, was the embodiment of the mantra 'less is more' and earned her the title 'the thinking woman's designer'. Sander's niche was providing the pared-down luxury wardrobe – combining seductive fabrics with a refined yet wearable silhouette. 'Even classical cuts need to be redefined again and again to look fresh and attractive,' she told the *New York Times*. 'I don't want to do away with trends. I am more interested in being consistent with my collection.' A former fashion writer, Sander had an educated overview of the industry before she entered it and cites Bauhaus architecture as a major influence. 'I find the same principles in perfection of all ages,' she explained, 'the same sense of proportion and symmetry, the same dedication to craftwork.'

Sander was always more interested in male than female attire. She analyzed the cuts, colours and quality of fabrics, feeling an affinity with the straightforwardness of menswear – a legacy that she admits has given her clothes an androgynous edge. 'I was always watching people, thinking how they could be made to look better,' she remembered. 'I had a very good eye.'

Her first Paris collection in 1973 was poorly received, but she persevered and found a market in both New York and London. Though she had no business partner or backer, Sander did not waver. 'I began thinking very pure, very minimalistic,' she said. *Manager Magazin* concluded: 'She has succeeded through sheer energy and egotism.'

The Sander look developed organically, starting with the finest Italian fabrics, meticulous manufacturing and impeccable finish. In 1993 Sander unveiled her four-storey Paris store on exactly the same site as Madeleine Vionnet (p. 29) had opened her first couture house. Sander was, by now, heading an empire with an estimated worth of nearly £150 million and with 232 boutiques worldwide. Priding herself on 'thinking and acting globally', she had healthy sales figures in America, although, as she told the *Sunday Times*: 'The European idea has always been motivating for me. I create fashion for women in Munich, Madrid, Paris, Milan, London, but also in New York, Hong Kong and Tokyo.' The Sander customer was international – a businesswoman, wife, mother – a grown-up female who had an aversion to fussiness and a desire for sophisticated understatement. Sander sums up her customers as 'women with confidence and class.'

Opposite Linda Evangelista's neutral toned coat and crossover dress exudes luxury and encapsulates Sander's ethos. Autumn/Winter 1991.

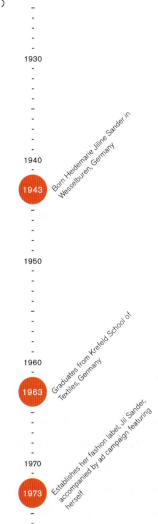

Opposite Clean lines, contemporary proportions, and detail subtly amended to make it modern. Spring/Summer 1995.

Above A generously cut coat with a gently extended shoulderline is paired with fluid trousers. 1992.

Right Sander (right) with a model at her her shop in 1968.

1920

1930

1940

1943 Born Heidemarie Jiline Sander in Wesselburen, Germany

1950

1960

1963 Graduates from Krefeld School of Textiles, Germany

1970

1973 Establishes her fashion label, Jil Sander, accompanied by ad campaign featuring herself

1980

1987 Presents her first runway show in Milan

1990

1993 Jil Sander boutique opens in Paris

1997 Launches Jil Sander Menswear collection

1999 The Prada group invests in a 75% stake in the company

2004 Resigns (following an earlier resignation four years earlier)

2010

2012 Returns to the company after the departure of Raf Simons, only to leave again the following year

'An outfit should be thrown together with aplomb and gay abandon.'

Tommy Nutter

1943–1992

UNITED KINGDOM

The flamboyant figure who revolutionized Savile Row in the 1960s, Tommy Nutter changed more than the cut of a man's suit. 'Before Nutters it was an exclusive closed-off world. They didn't even have window displays. Though, of course, the rest of the row looked upon him as an upstart whose shop was on the wrong side of the street,' said fashion curator Dennis Nothdruft. Cited by Tom Ford (p. 277) as a major influence, and dressing both Mick and Bianca Jagger, Nutter was the tailor of choice for the rock star, celebrity or aristocrat who wanted tailoring with a touch of subversion. He became the figurehead for a new, unstuffy attitude to bespoke, where lapels were larger, waists smaller and checks louder, and where colour palettes were anything but predictable. His window displays were equally surreal, with tuxedos tumbling out of rubbish bins surrounded by patchouli-soaked stuffed rats wearing diamond chokers. Large phallic purple candles embellished the windows.

In an era when Savile Row tailoring was a completely separate entity from fashion, Nutter drew a different, younger clientele to a rarefied area of London. Nutters opened its doors on Valentine's Day 1969, the interior decorated with chocolate-coloured carpets and mirrored walls.

Although Tommy Nutter was the figurehead, the Nutter revolution was actually a partnership. Nutter attracted the clients and drew the concept sketches, but it was a master tailor with consummate skill called Edward Sexton who made the designs a reality. Their early careers had been diametrically opposed – Nutter initially trained as a plumber before studying tailoring at the Tailor and Cutter Academy; Sexton had apprenticed

as a tailor. They met at Donaldson, Williamson & Ward in London's Burlington Arcade, making a pact to blow away the preconceived ideas of traditional men's tailoring.

Although he was dressing Hardy Amies and David Hockney, one of Nutter's proudest moments was providing suits for three of the four Beatles for their *Abbey Road* album cover (1969). A contemporary dandy often seen wearing an Edwardian coat, in 1971 Nutter was elected to the US Best Dressed List, with *American Menswear* commenting that he was 'tradition spiced with daring'. He branched out into ready-to-wear, expanding the business into East Asia.

Nutter's clients admired his easy charm but most of all his incredible insight. He was often called upon to advise on such intricate issues as the appropriate attire for a safari or the correct buttoning of a dinner suit. 'This knowledge extended to such minutiae as the correct wearing of half or full brogues or correspondent shoes,' recalled one of his clients. 'He was an encyclopaedia of correct, classical male style.'

Opposite Creating suits for Elton John on and off stage during the 1980s, Nutter dovetailed sharp tailoring with distinctive fabrication.

Below Proving his ability to produce flattering tailoring for both sexes, Nutter dressed both Bianca and Mick Jagger.

Opposite top The unconventional edging, accentuated proportions and off-centre coloration were typically Tommy Nutter. 1966.

Opposite bottom The cover of the Beatles' seminal *Abbey Road* album of 1969 featured three Nutter suits. Only George Harrison wore jeans.

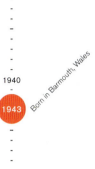

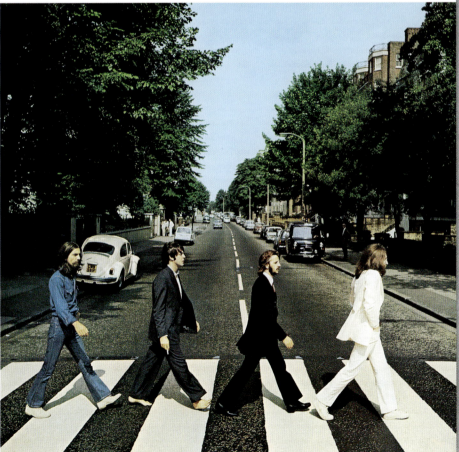

1920

1930

1940

1943 Born in Barmouth, Wales

1950

1958 Studies plumbing at Willesden Technical College

1960

1969 Forms his own business on Savile Row with tailor Edward Sexton

Elected to the Best Dressed List in the US

1971 Sexton buys Nutter out of the business; Nutter works for Kilgour, French and Stanbury on Savile Row, managing his own studio

1976 Signed for 5 years to Japanese conglomerate Daido Worsted Mills and Milliontex Corp.

1980 Establishes ready-to-wear shop called Tommy

1983 Nutter, Savile Row

1989 Creates costume for Jack Nicholson in *Batman* film

Dies in London, England

1992

2000

2010

'To be modern is to tear
the soul out of everything.'

Yohji Yamamoto

b. 1943

JAPAN

An enigmatic inventor whose name is synonymous with avant-garde fashion, Yohji Yamamoto has quietly made a stand against conformity for more than 30 years. His singular vision of beauty revels in imperfection and embraces the off-centre: 'I think perfection is ugly,' said Yamamoto in 2011. 'Somewhere in the things humans make, I want to see the scars, failure, disorder, distortion. Perfection is a kind of order. A free human being doesn't desire such things.'

Yamamoto's clothes attract the intelligentsia, creative thinkers who feel they have found common ground. First shown in Tokyo in 1977, Yamamoto's ready-to-wear 'Y' collection received rave reviews and secured him retail space in the Seibu department store. Outside Japan, the reception was different. In 1981, his Paris catwalk show, containing unconventional cutting and radical ideas coupled with expressionless faces, cropped hair and flat shoes, was a complete contradiction to the glitzy power-shouldered presentations of his contemporaries. Dubbed 'Hiroshima chic' and presented at the same time as Rei Kawakubo (p. 189), the show left the press puzzled and the buyers divided on whether this new vision was commercially viable. 'I had no intention of opposing the status quo,' Yamamoto stated in his 2010 autobiography, *My Dear Bomb*. 'I realized a line that just felt right to me, and the reaction split neatly into those who approved and those who did not. I took it all in my stride.'

Born in Tokyo at the end of World War II, Yamamoto credits his mother for bringing fashion to his attention. After completing a law degree at Keio University, Yamamoto shunned the corporate world and worked for his mother, who had a shop in the Kabukicho red-light district of Shinjuku, Tokyo. His inspiration was to create the antithesis of womanhood he had seen since childhood. 'I was determined, at all costs, to avoid creating the cute, doll-like women that some men so adore,' he said.

With a modest aim to 'open a tiny shop in Paris', he did not anticipate becoming a global brand. Although he adhered to seasonal deadlines, his clothes transcended the fashion calendar. 'Fashion is about what's next,' says Yamamoto. 'I wanted to do something that was timeless.' His androgynous aesthetic, his predominantly black palette, his penchant for futuristic fabrics, his inclusion of functional detail – all have meant that Yamamoto's collections are not only difficult to date but impossible to pigeonhole. He opened his first New York store in 1988, and the following year celebrated film director Wim Wenders attempted to explain Yamamoto's perspective in his documentary *Notebook on Cities and Clothes*.

In 2003, Yamamoto launched his pioneering Y-3 sportswear line for Adidas, but six years later he was rescued from bankruptcy by a private equity investor. 'I'm not so happy to be called a fashion designer. I hate fashion,' says Yamamoto. 'For a long time I was searching for a title for myself. Simply, I'm a dressmaker.'

Opposite Fearlessly exploring the possibilities of fashion and offering silhouettes that appeal to the avant garde. 2005.

Above Alternative bridalwear: a huge hooped skirt wider than the catwalk, headdress propped up with bamboo poles. Spring/Summer 1998.

Below Radical cutting techniques – most evident on the trousers – contrast with conventional buttoning at the top. Spring/Summer 1985.

Opposite A balancing act of tradition, asymmetry, curves, angles and a uniquely Japanese aesthetic. 1981.

Yohji Yamamoto

1920

1930

1940

1943 Born in Tokyo, Japan

1950

1955 Transfers from public school to the École de l'Étoile du Matin, Tokyo

1960

1966 Graduates from Tokyo's Keio University followed by Bunka Fashion College

1969 Wins So-en and Endo Fashion Awards; heads for Paris

1972 Yohji Yamamoto Inc. founded

1977 Paris debut

1980

1983 Opens in-store boutique in Charivari, New York

1988 Opens his first New York store

1989 *Notebook on Cities and Clothes* released – cinematic portrait of Yamamoto directed by Wim Wenders

1990 First Japanese designer to be awarded the Chevalier dans l'Ordre des Arts et des Lettres

1994 Starts collaborating with Adidas on capsule collection

2001 'Correspondences', the first of three retrospectives, opens in Florence followed by Antwerp and Paris

2005 Designs limited edition of fine jewellery

2007 'Yohji Yamamoto at the V&A' retrospective staged in London

2011 Re-issue of fragrances first formulated by Yamamoto in the 1990s

2014

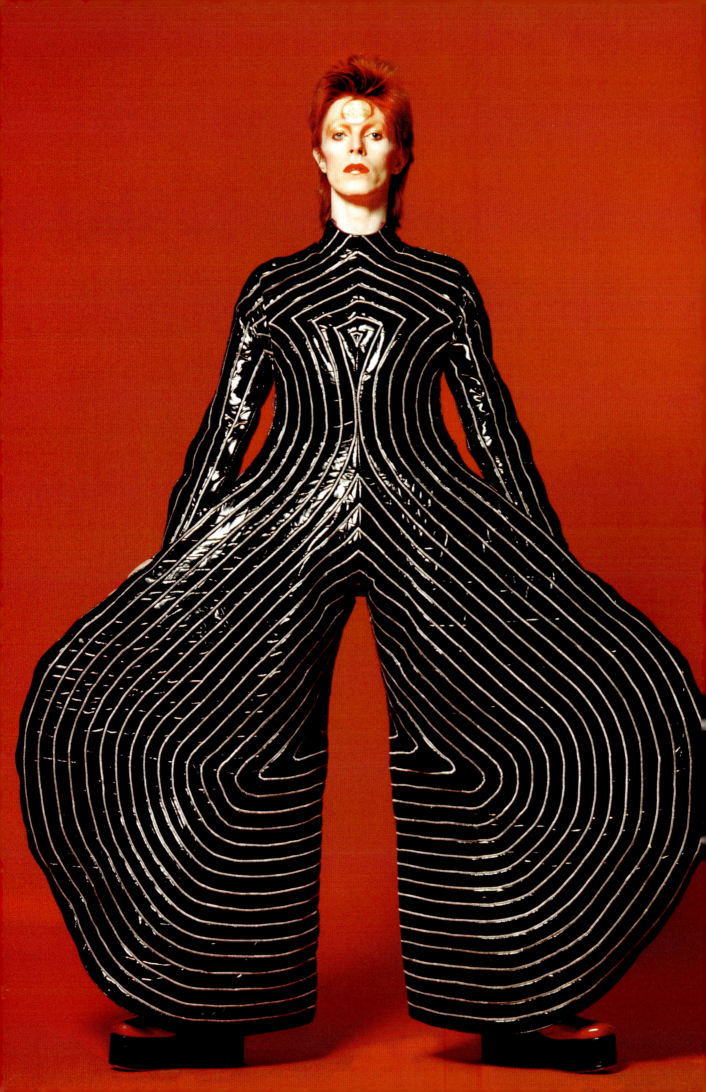

'There are no other designers doing what I do. My shows are how I feel at that exact moment in time.'

Kansai Yamamoto

b. 1944

JAPAN

'The first 20 years of my career I spent as a fashion designer, then the next 20 years I focused on entertainment. Now, for the first time I am combining those two,' Kansai Yamamoto told *Women's Wear Daily* in April 2013. At the forefront of the 1970s Japanese fashion invasion of the West, Kansai Yamamoto is perhaps most famous for dressing David Bowie. His colourful, theatrical designs, which mixed traditional Japanese kabuki costume with avant-garde ideas, captured the imagination of the ultimate image-conscious performer. They were also instrumental in forming the identity of Bowie's alter ego, Ziggy Stardust.

A natural showman and former student of English and engineering, Yamamoto was always torn between making clothes to be sold commercially and outfits whose primary role was to entertain an audience. Together with Issey Miyake (p. 169) and Hanae Mori, Yamamoto was part of the new wave of designers who cleverly combined the traditions of the Far East with contemporary thinking. He was the first Japanese designer to show in London and his presentation of 1971 was heralded by *Harpers & Queen* as 'The Show of the Year… a spectacular coup de théâtre'.

Yamamoto already had a boutique in Tokyo but he was poised to become an international name when his collection was spotted by David Bowie. 'My aim was to make clothes that nobody else was attempting,' Yamamoto explains. 'Costumes that would look great on artists who really want to express their individuality, not necessarily the general public.' In 1973, Yamamoto's designs were being worn by Bowie during the latter's

Ziggy Stardust tour – Bowie had chosen pieces from the womenswear collection to enable him to transcend gender. 'I like bright colours, and I like to stand out in a crowd. So I had a real empathy with Bowie,' said Yamamoto. 'He's from the West, I'm from the East, but we had the same crazy energy in our hearts. We inspired each other, and pushed each other to another level.' Yamamoto added John Lennon and Michael Jackson to his list of clients during the 1970s and 1980s.

His involvement on an aesthetic level with Bowie was the catalyst for a change in Yamamoto's approach. He became more of a producer than a fashion designer, creating 'Kansai Super Shows'. In 1981, 15,000 fans attended one of Yamamoto's fashion shows, while in total, approximately 3.5 million have been witness to the Kansai Super Show experience – which combines music, dance, entertainment and fashion on a grand scale – over the past 20 years. 'I've done everything I ever said I would,' said Yamamoto in 2014. 'Everything. And that's not going to change until I die.'

Opposite Yamamoto is forever fixed in the public consciousness for his Ziggy Stardust costumes commissioned by David Bowie.

Kansai Yamamoto

Opposite Enlarged, expressive illustrations from the Kabuki theatre are printed onto a button-through cape and flared dress. 1971.

Above Bold, multi-coloured shorts suits with a sportswear edge, in stretch jersey and quilted silk paired with platform and wedge boots. c. 1971.

Left Yamamoto took his unmistakable interpretation of Orientalism to New York in 1981.

1920

1930

1940

1944 Born in Yokohama, Japan

1950

1960

1964 Studies Civil Engineering and English at Nippon University

1968 Apprentices with Junko Koshino and Hosano

1971 Opens own company, Yamamoto Kansai Co. Ltd and first collection debuts in London

1973 Designs for David Bowie's Ziggy Stardust tour

1975 Shows collection in Paris

1977 Kansai boutique opens in Paris and wins Tokyo Fashion Editor's Award

1980

1990

1993 First Kansai Super Show in Moscow's Red Square, attracting a crowd of 120,000

1999 Revitalizes the kimono with Junko Koshino

2001 Launches eyewear line

2009 Yamamoto retrospective at Philadelphia Museum of Art

2013 Makes fashion comeback at the 19th New Britain Mask Festival, Kokopo, Papua New Guinea

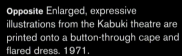

'You can find inspiration in everything. And if you can't, look again.'

Paul Smith

b. 1946

UNITED KINGDOM

With an eclectic mix of the quirky, the classic and the quintessentially British, Paul Smith has carved a unique niche in the global fashion market. His off-centre take on Englishness has captivated customers in 66 countries and made Smith one of the most financially successful British fashion designers in history. He is particularly popular in the Far East. Renowned for his idiosyncratic approach, Smith, like Ralph Lauren (p. 177), learned his trade on the shop floor. While Lauren sold ties, Smith sold suits, both building their business as a consequence of customer insight. He defines his role matter-of-factly as 'creating things for people to wear that make them feel good, feel special or are useful and hard-wearing'.

Smith left school at 15 to work in a clothing warehouse, but later tapped into his personal passions to organically grow the Paul Smith empire. An enthusiastic cyclist who harboured ambitions to win the Tour de France, he decided to change direction after a serious accident. Within two years Smith was managing Nottingham's first boutique. By now he had become a dandy, wearing a handmade pale pink suit and red python boots. In 1970, together with his girlfriend, Pauline Denyer, a design graduate of the Royal College of Art, Smith opened his own shop in Nottingham – in a tiny back room – called Paul Smith Vêtement Pour Homme, selling Kenzo (p. 173), Margaret Howell, and a few pieces designed by Paul Smith.

In 1993 Smith experienced a eureka moment when he discovered that although the majority of his clients were men, 15 per cent of his sales were to women. He decided to launch Paul Smith Women, a natural progression 'showing the honesty of my menswear with respect for the female form'. The new line joined Paul

Smith, PS, Paul Smith Jeans and Paul Smith Childrenswear. By this stage in his career, Paul Smith had an annual turnover of £54 million. Five years later this turnover had almost tripled. He received the Queen's Award for Industry in 1995.

Although Paul Smith is a global concern, it is in Tokyo that Smith has become an icon. 'It's like being a rock star,' he said. 'When I walk down the street, people ask me for autographs.' It was in Japan that Smith, a self-confessed hoarder, could really satisfy his urge for collecting. Paul Smith's office in London is an Aladdin's cave of curious paraphernalia, decorated with everything from piggy banks to talking wristwatches.

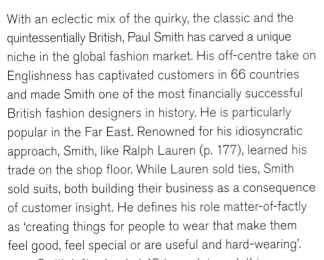

Opposite The English schoolgirl look made quirkier and more contemporary with monochrome colouring and defined outlines. 2007.

Left Florals are a recurring theme, often mixed with stripes, frequently appearing in menswear and accessories. 2004.

Below Eclectic but not elitist, the menswear collection contains traditional points of reference but adds an air of English eccentricity. 2008.

Paul Smith

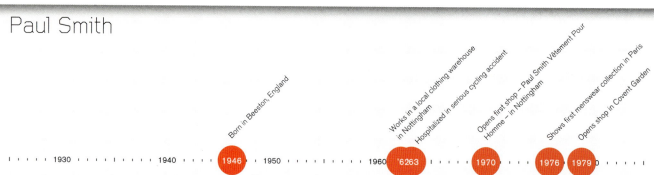

Born in Beeston, England

Works in a local clothing warehouse in Nottingham

Hospitalized in serious cycling accident

Opens first shop – Paul Smith Vêtement Pour Homme – in Nottingham

Shows first menswear collection in Paris

Opens shop in Covent Garden

1930 1940 **1946** 1950 1960 **'62 63** **1970** **1976 1979**

When Paul Smith was invited to reinterpret the Mini he simply embellished it with his signature stripe. 1999.

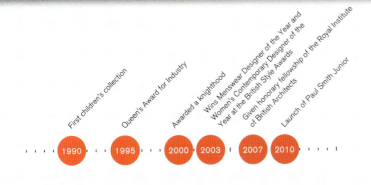

First children's collection
Queen's Award for Industry
Awarded a knighthood
Wins Menswear Designer of the Year and Women's Contemporary Designer of the Year at the British Style Awards
Given honorary fellowship of the Royal Institute of British Architects
Launch of Paul Smith Junior

1990 1995 2000 2003 2007 2010

'Design came to me.
I didn't have to move.'

Gianni Versace

1946–1997

ITALY

In the way only Italians can, Gianni Versace brought excess, glamour and palatial retail proportions to the fashion arena. Expert in overstating the obvious, he created exuberant clothes that celebrated curves, enhanced undulations and often left little to the imagination. He was instrumental in promoting the concept of the supermodel via his shows in the 1990s.

Long before celebrities were dabbling in design, Versace implicitly understood the link between the front row and fashion, courting and catering for a wide spectrum of rock stars, Oscar winners, musicians and royalty. His clientele ranged from Elton John to David Bowie, Elizabeth Hurley to Diana, Princess of Wales. The Medusa's head was Versace's signature symbol.

Often citing the prostitutes in his impoverished childhood home of Reggio di Calabria as his earliest influence, Versace would reconfigure these indelible images of sexuality into his illustration of luxury. 'If my mother hadn't made such a big deal about covering my eyes every time we passed a brothel, I wouldn't have developed such an interest in this look,' he was to say later. Versace studied architecture before switching to fashion at 26 years old, observing: 'It is very close, architecture and fashion. Good fashion is pure form. Not complicated.'

In 1972, Versace moved to Tuscany to design for a company called Florentine Flowers, before moving again to Milan. By the mid-1970s he was specializing in knitwear, securing freelance contracts with Genny and Callaghan. In 1975 he made his name by designing a collection for Complice. Basking in the first flush of success, with the help of his brother, Santo, Versace

formed his own label, telling *Vogue* in 1977 that he was creating 'a fashion that is alive. Dresses that move.' The following year, he opened his first boutique on Via della Spiga in Milan and presented his first collection at Milan's Permanente art gallery.

As the 1980s progressed, the Versace identity became embedded in the public consciousness. By 1989, Versace was also showing a couture collection in Paris. There were by then 320 outlets around the world. Versace did not rest on his laurels: his creative energy and chameleon qualities enabled him to design costumes for opera, ballet and the theatre. 'There is not only one Versace,' he said in 1990. 'There is a Versace who is very conservative, there is a Versace who is very crazy, there is a Versace who is very rock, there is a Versace who is very theatre. I haven't decided yet which I choose to be.'

Opposite Clashing prints, but a subtler than standard Italian colour spectrum broadened the brand's appeal. Autumn/Winter 1991.

Above Elizabeth Hurley made global headlines at the UK premiere of *Four Weddings and a Funeral* dressed in Versace's safety-pin dress. 1994.

Opposite Versace's passion for modern art and abstract pattern are echoed in a strapless beaded dress with short bouffant skirt. Spring/Summer 1991.

Gianni Versace

1920

1930

1940

1946 Born in Reggio di Calabria, Italy

1950

1955 Under the supervision of his dressmaker mother, he makes his first dress

1960

1970

1972 Relocates to Tuscany to work with knitwear company Florentine Flowers before moving to Milan

1978 Forms his own company; opens first boutique on Via della Spiga, Milan; launches menswear

1980

1983 'Gianni Versace: A Decade of Creativity' exhibition opens in Verona

1989 Opens Atelier Versace, presenting his first couture collection; launches Versus, his diffusion line

1990

1994 Elizabeth Hurley wears his safety-pin dress

1997 Murdered on the steps of his mansion at Miami Beach, Florida, USA

2000

2002 Honoured with a retrospective exhibition at London's Victoria & Albert Museum

2010

'I don't just see one woman when I design. It's always a universe of women.'

Donna Karan

b. 1948

UNITED STATES

'I design from instinct,' declared Donna Karan. 'It's the only way I know how to live.' With an approach to dressing women that focused on flattery and pivoted on the formulaic, Karan's opening mantra was: 'Delete the negative, accentuate the positive.' Taking lengths of luxurious fabrics and a predominantly black palette, Karan launched her version of the wearable wardrobe in autumn 1985. It was the result of 14 years of experience at Anne Klein, where she learned the art of dovetailing the desirable and the practical. Containing an interchangeable selection of jersey skirts, wrap coats and stretch bodies, the collection was titled 'Seven Easy Pieces' and was later dubbed 'system dressing'.

Karan's debut collection was the antithesis of the sharp-shouldered power suit. Her dream customer was the well-heeled executive who wanted to celebrate her curves, and Karan became her own best advertisement. 'I'm a woman with a rounded figure. I'm not a model size 8. I won't design clothes that can't be worn by a woman who is a size 12 or 14.'

Karan's statement on business dress instantly caught the imagination of the female careerist whose ambition was to portray a polished persona infused with sex appeal. It was essentially a New York look that translated internationally. When she opened her store on London's Bond Street in 1996 she admitted, 'It's a pretty global look. It's a life I live and breathe and I think that London is absolutely 100 per cent going to be great for us.'

Karan's pioneering approach was partly due to her parentage. She grew up on New York's Long Island, her father a custom tailor, her mother a fashion model whom Karan described as 'Dorothy Lamour, Susan Hayward and Ann Miller all rolled into one'. Initially wanting to be a fashion illustrator, Karan attended Parsons Design School, but dropped out before graduation. At 18 years old she interned at Anne Klein and rose through the ranks to become head designer. In May 1985 she launched her first collection under her own label. It was greeted with a standing ovation. *Vogue* reported simply: 'Donna Karan has arrived.' The tabloids called Karan 'The Woman Who Reshaped America'. The 'Seven Easy Pieces' collection became the bestselling label in the United States that year, with customers relating to Karan's philosophy that 'I needed a wardrobe, a real clear defined wardrobe that would take me from day into evening'.

In 1991 Karan introduced menswear, approaching it with the same vision as her womenswear line. 'For me, the quest of design lies in problem-solving. What's missing, how can I fill the gap?' In 2002 she was inducted into the Fashion Walk of Fame.

Opposite Offering the opposite to the sharp-shouldered suit, this was a debut collection that encapsulated ease. 1985.

'Five Easy Pieces'. The foundation of
system dressing started with the body,
designed with or without sleeves. 1985.

Donna Karan

1920

1930

1940

1948 Born Donna Ivy Faske in New York

1950

1960

1966 Studies at Parsons School of Design

1970 Becomes Associate Designer of Anne Klein

1974 On the death of Anne Klein, Karan is appointed head designer

1980

1985 Establishes her own company 'Donna Karan New York' in Halston's former offices; 'Seven Easy Pieces' becomes a bestseller

1991 Wins CFDA's Womenswear Designer of the Year Award and launches menswear line

2001 LVMH purchases the Donna Karan company
2002 Inducted into the Fashion Walk of Fame

2004 Receives Lifetime Achievement Award from CFDA

2009 Launches jeans line

'I have always tried to
sublimate the body and
to make people dream.'

Thierry Mugler

b. 1948

FRANCE

'I don't believe in natural fashion,' stated Mugler in 1994. 'Let's go for it! The corset, the push-up bra. Everything! If we do it, let's do the whole number.' His signature cinched waists and exaggerated shoulders symbolized 1980s power dressing. Whether it was wearing a Plexiglass sex suit or moulding her curves in plastic, the Mugler woman had no qualms about cosmetic touches, no limits on sartorial enhancement. His catwalk shows were legendary for their showmanship. 'I don't do easy clothes,' he admitted, 'because looking good isn't easy. When you start to have shape, you feel stronger. My clothes exude power and sensuality and influence.'

Mugler was born in Strasbourg, France. His father was a doctor, and his mother was described by her son as 'the most elegant woman in town'. Attending Strasbourg's School of Decorative Arts, Mugler joined the corps de ballet of the Rhine Opera, where he remained for six years. At the age of 20, he moved to Paris to find a contemporary dance company and worked for the Gudule boutique as a designer and window dresser. By now he was starting to make his own clothes. 'They were very colourful,' he recalled. 'I had an old army coat which trailed on the ground and a pair of trousers dyed in all colours of the rainbow.'

His first collection, presented in 1973, was called 'Café de Paris'. In 1976, helped by fashion editor Melka Tréanton, Mugler showed his work in Japan. By 1978 Mugler had opened his first Paris boutique on the Place des Victoires and launched a fashion collection for men. He hired Helmut Newton to photograph his first advertising campaign, but took over when they fell out. 'I was furious that somebody should tell me how to take

my photos,' said Newton, suggesting that Mugler take his own. This he did.

During the 1980s, the Mugler brand grew from sales of 5 million francs in 1981 to 162 million a decade later. Mugler celebrated 20 years in the industry by presenting 300 looks on 120 models, broadcast live on French television. Publishing his retrospective in 1998 he said in it: 'Fashion, it's wonderful and very cruel: a very demanding mistress.' He made his exit from mainstream fashion at the end of his July 2000 couture show, but he was lured back into the industry as the decade progressed. His signature style had always bordered on costume rather than wearable clothing. He designed costumes for the Cirque du Soleil in 2003, and six years later was commissioned by Beyoncé for her world tour, after she had seen his iconic designs in the Met's Costume Institute 'Superheroes' show the year before. He did not restrict himself to costume design alone for the tour, getting involved in the sets, the lighting and the footage shown on stage. 'I never considered myself a fashion designer,' he said. 'Never.'

Opposite Inspired by insects, a sinous silhouette and an element of showmanship. Autumn/Winter 1998.

Below Mugler's vision of an alluring fashion siren is often personified by model Jerry Hall. 1994.

Opposite A cross between a goddess and a vamp, this typical piece of fantastical eveningwear exaggerates and enhances. 1995.

Thierry Mugler

1920

1930

1940

1948 Born in Strasbourg, France

1950

1962 Attends Strasbourg's School of Decorative Arts; joins the corps de ballet of the Rhine Opera

1960

1970

1973 Having been a freelance designer in Paris, Milan, Barcelona and London, Mugler presents his own collection called 'Café de Paris'

1978 Launches menswear collection

1980

1984 Staging of Mugler's seminal show at Le Zenith concert hall, Paris

1992 His creations appear in George Michael music video; creates his debut scent, 'Angel'

1990

1997 Mugler company bought by Clarins

2000

2003 Designs costumes for Cirque du Soleil's show 'Zumanity' in Las Vegas

2007 Cosmetics collection 'Art of Metamorphosis' launched

2010

2013 Mugler resigns as artistic director of his company, but remains as a consultant

'Fashion now plays more on the personality than true talent. It's showmanship.'

Claude Montana

b. 1949

FRANCE

Extreme and unmistakable, the Montana silhouette was a sharp series of undulations that started with an elongated shoulder, tapered midway to a tiny waist and ended with a narrow skirt – an outline that was constantly imitated during its heyday. Montana's fantasy woman was fearless, a vampish female who, according to him, 'didn't care about comfort, just about her look'. Making the transition from jewellery to fashion design, Montana – along with Azzedine Alaïa (p. 181) and Thierry Mugler (p. 229) – became one of the key names of the 1980s. Themes at his catwalk extravaganzas ranged from the fall of the Roman Empire to Sicilian widows. 'It might have been fun on the runway but it was crazy,' remembered Montana, who was once called 'the most gifted creator of his generation'.

Born in Paris to a German mother and Catalan father, Montana decamped to London at the age of 20 when his family found it unacceptable that he wanted a career in fashion. Struggling to survive and sleeping in fashion photographer Hans Feurer's studio, Montana made a collection of papier-mâché jewellery studded with rhinestones, which ended up being featured in British *Vogue*. Returning to France he worked as a freelance illustrator before taking up a position with leather company MacDouglas. It was here that he learned about the precise treatment of skins and complex construction techniques that were to play a formative role in his later collections. 'I have learnt a lot of things,' he commented, 'but I don't sew or cut patterns.'

Introducing his own line in 1976, Montana was not an instant hit. 'At first I was very well received by the press but not by the buyers,' he recalled. The hard-edged look of his first major catwalk collection the following year, however, caught the imagination of both. Black leather suits, sometimes accessorized with peaked caps,

featuring epaulettes and decorated with chains, became the seminal Montana look. His single-mindedness and lack of retrospection was refreshing, and he was described as being 'like a sharply focused laser beam'.

But the applause did not last. He turned down the post of creative director at Christian Dior (p. 73) but in 1990 he was employed by Lanvin (p. 21) to reinvigorate the house. Montana's first collection was panned, dismissed as looking 'like a graduating art student's efforts made up by his mom', but the subsequent collections were praised.

Although he was the recipient of two consecutive Golden Thimble awards and the creator of a new State of Montana diffusion line, this was not sufficient to save the house he founded. Openly homosexual, Montana caused a scandal when he married his model and muse Wallis Franken in the middle of couture week in the summer of 1993. Three years later, she committed suicide by throwing herself from their Paris apartment window. In 1997 Montana filed for bankruptcy.

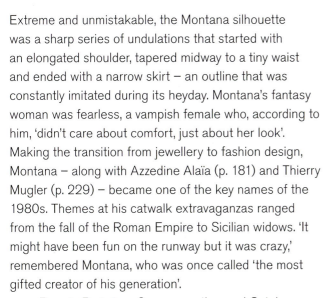

Opposite Sharp, clean, always accentuating the waist and featuring vampish detailing. Autumn/Winter 1995.

STREIFENPOPELINEBLUSE
M. GOLDKNÖPFEN

103

ROCK HINTEN

DEUX - PIECES AUS BEDRUCKTEM C.D.C.

LEINENANZÜGE AUS BLUSE / CORSAIRE / LG. JACKE
ODER MIT LANGHOSEN-OVERALL , ODER , ODER . . . !
GRAU / MIMOSE , PECHE / TÜRKIS , GOLDNÄGEL

NOCH EINE JACKEN-
FORM , WEISS PIKEE

103

WEISSE LEINEN-
JACKE ZU
SCHWARZEM
LEINENKLEID
M. SCHWARZEM
ORGANZA-
PLISSEESCHOSS

ÜBER SAMTIG SCHWAR-
ZEN OVERALLS
BLUMENFARBENE
NYLON-SATINMÄNTEL
FEUER OD. KROKUS

Claude Montana

1920

1930

1940

1949 Born in Paris, France

1960

1970

Designs biker leathers for French company
MacDouglas

1974 Creates 'House of Montana'

1979 Montana Hommes, his first menswear collection, debut

1981 Opens Paris boutique

1983 Launches first fragrance 'Montana'

1986 Designs couture for the House of Lanvin, receiving two
consecutive Golden Thimble Awards

1990 'State of Claude Montana' line designed

1992 Montana BLU launched – affordable
womenswear line

1999 Having filed for bankruptcy previously, presents
his last Paris show

2002 Claude Montana: Fashion Radical published

2011

Opposite top and bottom The ultra-wide shoulder, cinched waist, voluminous flare and vampish look all feature in these illustrations of Montana's work drawn by Hannelore Bruederlin. Spring/Summer 1980.

Above Multicoloured menswear is here inspired by the street with a reference to 1950s teddy boy style. 1995.

Right The classic fetish fantasy: leather overcoat and stiletto boots, worn with a sheer bodysuit underneath. 1983.

'I'm not interested in types. I'm interested in archetypes.'

Miuccia Prada

b. 1949

ITALY

The only fashion designer to possess a doctorate in political science, Miuccia Prada is also a self-confessed 'leftist feminist', an ex-Communist and a major player in the contemporary art world. Her intellectual approach and visionary outlook have turned an ailing luxury goods company into a global empire. In 2014, with an estimated net worth of $10.4 billion, the Prada family was listed as one of the richest in the world. Miuccia Prada's fatalistic attitude contradicts preconceived ideas about brand-building. 'I want Prada to be successful but the idea of the brand doesn't interest me,' she said. 'I never think about it.'

Part of the 1960s generation that believed in feminist ideals and the power of political activism, Miuccia Prada originally trained as a mime artist. Joining the Prada family business, established in 1913, was not on her agenda. 'Being so involved in the women's movement then, and everything that it was trying to accomplish, I thought that making bags or shoes or dresses was the worst way I could spend my time,' she told the London *Evening Standard*.

After meeting her husband Patrizio Bertelli, the owner of a Tuscan leather-goods factory, she did, however, become a fashion designer. With a renewed seriousness about the Prada business, Miuccia introduced women's footwear, and then created the item which was to change everything: the Prada nylon backpack. Launched in 1984 and constructed from the same heavyweight material as used by the Italian army, this black waterproof bag paved the way for the designer handbag revolution. With its triangular signature logo and card verifying its authenticity, it went on to be a worldwide hit.

Prada's success lay in her extraordinary ability to predict cultural shifts. 'For me, it's important to anticipate where fashion is heading,' she said. Her starting point was primarily instinctive, designing something she personally liked but also considering pertinent issues, such as 'why people like something, trying to find a way to look at it from outside, researching new ideas on beauty and femininity and the way it is perceived in contemporary culture'.

Prada's secondary line, Miu Miu, was launched in 1993 as a younger, more subversive take on the Prada signature. 'It's about the bad girls I knew at school, the ones I envied,' she told *Time*. The Miuccia Prada mystique intact, she continues to be involved in artistic projects, including a travelling exhibition of 100 of her skirt designs, plus costume designs for Verdi's *Attila* at the Metropolitan Opera, New York, and for Baz Luhrmann's 2013 film adaptation of *The Great Gatsby*.

Opposite The youthful exuberance of Prada's design mantra mixes snakeskin boots with a bold graphic shift, worn here by actress Kaya Scodelario. 2011.

Opposite The delicate femininity of rococo lace is made modern and paired with futuristic sunglasses. 2008.

Above Embellishment inspired by the 1960s is brought into the twenty-first century by reworking the shaping. 2004.

Below The classic nylon Prada backpack that triggered the 1990s trend for the designer accessory.

Miuccia Prada

1920

1930

1940

1949 Born in Milan, Italy

1960

1970

1977 Takes over family business Fratelli Prada, founded in 1913

1980

1982 Launch of women's footwear line; opens new store on Milan's Via Della Spiga

1984 Introduces a black nylon backpack which becomes an iconic accessory

1988 Womenswear collection designed

1990

1993 Secondary line Miu Miu introduced, followed by men's ready-to-wear shoes and accessories

1996 Flagship store opens on New York's Madison Avenue

2000

2003 Tokyo store opens and reports 3,500 visitors in the first weekend

2008 First fashion designer to make the cover of the New York *Times Magazine*

2010

2012 'Schiaparelli and Prada: Impossible Conversations' exhibition opens at the Metropolitan Museum of Art, New York

'It's easy to be funny with a T-shirt, but it's more clever with a mink coat.'

Franco Moschino

1950–1994

ITALY

Frequently called 'the clown prince of fashion', Franco Moschino was known for bringing humour and irreverence to a world that often takes itself far too seriously. His lack of pretension was refreshing. 'I'm not a fashion designer,' he told the *New York Times* in 1991. 'I'm a painter, a decorator. I'm not the author of a new era.' Moschino's sense of fun and aptitude for one-liners was coupled with his capacity to send up the seriously expensive designer brands. He designed a parody of the Chanel suit with the words 'Waist of Money' where the signature gold chain should be. Moschino's sense of the ridiculous extended to himself. He appeared in advertising campaigns in a variety of guises including Popeye and a transvestite. His company motto was 'Fashion is full of chic.' 'My approach is a contradiction, I know,' he admitted to the *Sunday Times* in 1993. 'But why should I have to embrace the fashion business just because I work in it?'

Born into a traditional family in rural northern Italy, Moschino could have followed his family into their iron foundry business. Instead he headed for Milan, where he studied ceramics, life-drawing and scenography at the Accademia di Belle Arti. While working as a fashion illustrator he was spotted by Gianni Versace (p. 221). 'My uncle wasn't happy with it at all, but he changed his mind when I became successful.'

Moschino's first designer job was in 1976 for an Italian ready-to-wear company called Cadette, where he designed its collections for 11 seasons. He founded his own company, Moonshadow, and launched the Moschino Couture! label in 1983. Five years later, he presented the more affordable Cheap and Chic line, which although at a lower price point was still impeccably made. Humour apart, Moschino was heavily influenced by the Surrealist movement, with a style that also had shades of Elsa Schiaparelli (p. 45). He decorated a dinner suit with real cutlery, designed a bodice that consisted entirely of gold safety pins on a strapless dress, and produced a skirt constructed from rows of zip fastenings. 'It's all a matter of weight,' he explained. 'You can make a teacup and use it as an earring. We have the right to use *anything* to decorate ourselves.'

Moschino himself was surprised by his success, particularly in his homeland, with its tradition of taking fashion very seriously. Opening his first shop in 1989 on Via Sant'Andrea, Milan, the statistics were starting to add up: 23 lines (including underwear, jewellery and jeans), and an annual turnover of £450 million. 'The store will be another way of communicating,' he said. 'Not necessarily fashion, this is not important to me, it will communicate love, fun, happiness – whatever you want.' In 1991 Moschino replaced catwalk presentations with private showings. 'My sense of humour is driven by a sense of drama,' he said. 'I'm a typical Italian.'

Opposite Continuing in the tradition of causing a stir, Moschino suggests a couple of naughty nuns on the catwalk. Spring/Summer 2014.

Opposite Statements, question marks, scribbles and symbols randomly adorn a Moschino jacket and T-shirt. Spring/Summer 1994.

Above Characteristically Moschino: A prim and proper polka-dot blouse and strict skirt accessorized with a watering can. Spring/Summer 1987.

1920

1930

1940

1950 Born in Abbiategrasso, Italy

1960

1968 Studies fine art at the Accademia di Belle Arti, Milan

1971 Becomes an illustrator for Gianni Versace

1980

1983 Founds his own company, Moonshadow, followed by Moschino Couture!

1985 Launches men's collection

1988 Introduces 'Cheap & Chic' diffusion line; publishes Moschino. To Be, or Not to Be, That's Fashion!

1990

1994 Dies in Milan, Italy, having presented his last eco-friendly collection earlier that year

2000

2010

'The world needs some
excitement from fashion.'

Christian Lacroix

b. 1951

FRANCE

'Vive Lacroix! There's been nothing like it for 25 years,' declared the cover of the *Sunday Times Magazine* on 4 October 1987, heralding the first new Paris couture debut for a quarter of a century. Christian Lacroix, then a 36-year-old fashion designer from Arles, was responsible for what was described as 'the fashion event of the generation'. He was applauded unanimously and internationally, the *New York Times* reporting, 'We've had nothing like this since Dior and Saint Laurent. A new star? A new king!'

Making a swift exit from Jean Patou, where he had been design director since 1981, Lacroix was given a salon, a £5 million investment, and free rein to concoct a delicious sartorial spectacle that would form the base for a lucrative luxury brand. 'Couture is the umbrella that brings legitimacy to the money-spinning ventures then created under its name and aura,' explained Lacroix's backer and new financial director, Bernard Arnault. 'The couture, as Christian Lacroix is brilliantly equipped to create it, projects the dream, the drama, the big powerful fashion statement.'

A fashion historian at heart, Lacroix studied art history and, intending to become a museum curator, he wrote his thesis on eighteenth-century clothing. His talent came to the fore when he joined Jean Patou, employed, according to Patou's nephew, for his 'complete knowledge of the past'. He presented a Spanish-themed collection in 1985, which had the *New York Times* already claiming Lacroix was 'the savior of the couture world'.

Lacroix's clothes appealed primarily to the monied American and eccentric European markets. Even before he embarked on his first couture collection, Lacroix was the recipient of two Golden Thimble awards. In April 1987 Lacroix's salon opened in a nineteenth-century building off the rue du Faubourg Saint-Honoré. On 26 July of that year, the collection was ready to be presented to the public. 'I wanted magic, a wonderland of fashion, and also a serious theatre of fashion,' said Lacroix at the opening. By 1990 Lacroix had featured on three *Vogue* covers and launched his perfume C'est la Vie. However, the sensational press coverage was not enough to secure the future of Lacroix's company and his fragrance – the financial lifeblood of any couture brand – flopped.

From 2002 to 2005 Lacroix worked as creative director of the Italian fashion house Emilio Pucci. He went on producing exquisite couture pieces until he filed for bankruptcy in May 2009. After the closure of his salon, Lacroix continued to create – primarily interiors, but also collaborating with Barcelona-based clothing brand Desigual.

Opposite Exuberant use of colour, amazing attenton to detail, and always unashamedly theatrical. Autumn/Winter 1991.

Christian Lacroix

Opposite La Corrida dress: key influences here are the matador costume along with the paintings and palette of Pablo Picasso. Autumn/Winter 1987.

Left Based on a mini version of the bustle, this 'pouf' or bubble skirt was one of the seminal looks for 1987.

Leaves Patou to launch his own couture house, backed by Bernard Arnault

Pieces of a Pattern: Lacroix by Lacroix published

Launches Christian Lacroix Jeans

Creates his debut collection for Emilio Pucci

Opens Hotel du Petit Moulin in Paris; shows final collection for Pucci

Files for bankruptcy before presenting his final couture show

1987 · 1990 1992 · 1996 · · 2000 2002 2005 · · 2009 · · · ·

'I'm still astounded by some
people's reactions to things
I consider quite normal.'

Jean Paul Gaultier

b. 1952

FRANCE

'I feel much too old to be an enfant terrible,' a 34-year-old Jean Paul Gaultier told the *Times* in 1986. Almost 30 years later he is still causing a stir, reportedly quipping to model Carla Bruni: 'My favourite piece of clothing is a condom.' Provocative, ironic, amusing, with particular expertise in the art of androgyny, Gaultier has never confined himself to the catwalk. Recently appointed Diet Coke's creative director, Gaultier has also been a television chat show host, costume designer and recording artist. He was the first fashion designer in history to be elected to the jury for the Cannes Film Festival. In sartorial terms, he became infamous for putting men in skirts and women in conical bras. The classic Breton stripe is his signature style.

'I started fashion from a movie,' says Gaultier, who cites the 1945 film *Falbalas*, set in the world of Paris fashion, as 'an enormous influence on my life'. With a stylish grandmother for his earliest inspiration, as an infant he created his first cone bra on a teddy bear and at 9 years old was drawing fantasy costumes for the Folies Bergère in the classroom. Without any formal training in design, and shelving a fleeting fancy to be a pastry chef, Gaultier capitalized on his ability to produce engaging drawings. He sent illustrations to a host of Paris couturiers and was hired on his eighteenth birthday by Pierre Cardin (p. 105).

In his debut collection in 1979 Gaultier opted for blatant artificiality, later explaining: 'I was very naive. All I wanted to do was the opposite of the very loose clothes that were being made.' His opening gambit was a homage to man-made textures, with the fabrication summed up as 'everything shiny, stretchy and false'.

The 1980s undoubtedly were Gaultier's golden years, as he repeatedly delighted the fashion pundits with his unpredictable antics. He ended the decade with a double whammy – he was commissioned to design costumes for Peter Greenaway's film *The Cook, The Thief, His Wife and Her Lover* (1989), as well as the wardrobe for Madonna's Blond Ambition tour. During the 1990s he continued to push the boundaries, co-hosting a risqué TV show called *Eurotrash* and presenting a 'Chic Rabbis' collection, about which *Le Figaro* concluded: 'If you're mixing aesthetics and politics it's a dangerous line'. He was offered the top spot at Givenchy but turned it down with the words, 'I thought it was very bourgeois'.

Gaultier opened his own couture house in 1997, content in the knowledge he had changed the course of fashion history. 'There is a lot of conservatism coming into fashion,' he said. 'I'm quite sad about that.'

Opposite Madonna wears Gaultier's iconic satin conical corsetry, with elasticated panels, commissioned for her Blond Ambition world tour in 1990.

Above The original enfant terrible applies timeless Gaultier ingredients to the Hermès template (note the leather corset). Autumn/Winter 2004.

Left 'Her look was incredible – with her sailor tattoos she was so Gaultier!' said the designer, paying homage to the late Amy Winehouse in his Paris couture show of 2012.

Opposite Layered organza panels of varying depth, fluting to the floor, inspired by English punk and French can-can. Haute couture, Spring/ Summer 2011.

Jean Paul Gaultier

1920

1930

1940

1950

1952 Born in Arcueil, France

1960

1970

1974 Having worked briefly for Pierre Cardin and Jean Patou, Gaultier is re-employed by Cardin in Manila

1979 Debut collection

1984 First haute couture collection for men

1988 Launch of the first 'Junior Gaultier' collection

1990

1992 First 'Gaultier Jeans' collection coincides with retrospective in Los Angeles

1997 Debut Haute Couture collection

2001 Awarded Chevalier de la Legion d'Honneur

2003 Makes his debut as Design Director of Hermès

2011 'The Fashion World of Jean Paul Gaultier' exhibition opens at Montreal Museum of Fine Arts and travels to London in 2014

'The reality of fashion is to go to Paris. The mountain cannot come to you.'

Helmut Lang

b. 1956

AUSTRIA

Called a 'creative contradiction' and the 'most copied designer of his generation', Helmut Lang presented an avant-garde aesthetic in an era of exaggerated shoulderpads. He arrived on the international fashion scene in the 1980s with his unadorned and often androgynous look. The Lang label equalled edgy, urban and cool. Although his style was resolutely futuristic, it retained the human element, merging innovative fabrics with an inherent sensuality. 'The most important and intriguing thing about fashion is that it relates to people immediately in a very short time frame,' he said in 2004. 'It is an expression and a reaction. It's a reflection, even a proposal, on the current situation of our society.'

Lang opened his original studio in Vienna with a handful of seamstresses and rolls of inexpensive fabric, mainly polyester. He proceeded to stage a Paris show in 1986, which he summed up in retrospect as 'naive, crazy; you can only do this if you're young, inexperienced and have no idea of the consequences'. It coincided with the Belgian contingent unleashing their brand of deconstruction on the international catwalks (see Dries Van Noten, p. 265). Lang's collections, however, had a darker undercurrent. Typified by a fetishistic lace-and-rubber sheath, summed up by the *Times* as a style that 'spoke of sex in clubs or bars or somewhere dark and dangerous', it was counterpointed by glamorous wool coats and sequinned dresses. *Vogue*, refusing to categorize him, said he was 'at once a classicist and a minimalist'.

By the mid-1990s Lang was taking an anti-brand stance – he believed that the quality of the garment was more important than a conspicuous label. His innovative blending of high-tech and traditional fabrics was equalled with his visionary attitude to the Internet. Three days before his New York show in April 1998, he presented it live on the Internet – a first in the fashion industry.

In 2005, after 30 years in fashion, Lang decided to leave the industry. Wanting his legacy to be preserved, he dispersed almost his entire archive to contemporary art, design and fashion collections. After a fire in his studio building, he destroyed the remaining 6,000 pieces and used them as raw material for his 2011 art installation *Make It Hard*. His archive, almost in its entirety, survives in digital form. 'The human body is not the centre of attention any more,' muses Lang. 'It is more the human condition that is taking centre stage.'

Opposite Defining the urban dress code with sheer fabrication, black straps and skinny pants. Spring/Summer 2003.

Helmut Lang

Born in Vienna, Austria

1910   1920   1930   1940   1950   **1956**   1960

Opposite Experimental, abstract shift dress suspended from sheer straps, Autumn/Winter 1992.

Above left Translucent fabrics and stategically positioned seamlines with the mimimum of decoration. 1985.

Left Neutral colours, multiple layers, military straps and an air of ease. 2003.

Above Pared-down slimline suits develop the minimalist design aesthetic that defined the 1990s. Autumn/Winter 2000.

n-taught, Lang starts to make clothes for himself, later producing pieces bought by friends

Opens made-to-measure shop

Makes his Paris debut as part of Viennese showcase at the Centre Pompidou

Designs limited edition bag for Louis Vuitton

Becomes first international designer to show his collection live online

Prada buys 100% stake in Lang, retaining Lang as Creative Director

Debuts as a fine artist in Brooklyn

Shows installation made from 6,000 shredded garments from his own archive

1974   1979 0   1986   1990   1996 '98 000   2004 2007 20 2011

'Hats are a great antidote to what's going on. It's really their purpose to put a happy face on a sad world.'

Stephen Jones

b. 1957

UNITED KINGDOM

'Millinery is the punctuation of fashion,' states Stephen Jones definitively. 'We provide the apostrophes, the question marks, the exclamation marks.' The former punk and New Romantic has been eloquently dressing heads since 1980. His hats, commissioned by everyone from Karl Lagerfeld (p. 157) to Comme des Garçons (see Rei Kawakubo, p. 189), Marc Jacobs (p. 285) to John Galliano (p. 273), add the final flourish to countless catwalk collections. The list of collaborations throughout his career is a virtual A to Z of fashion, criss-crossing the globe from couture to ready-to-wear.

Inventiveness and imagination are his hallmarks. Jones has designed everything from a human hair hat for Nicolas Ghesquière's first collection at Balenciaga (p. 53) to a floral bathing cap for Anna Piaggi, the legendary editor of Italian *Vogue*. Piaggi called him 'the maker of the most beautiful hats in the world'. Jones's private clients have included the singers Grace Jones, Diana Ross and Barbra Streisand, and in 2005 he created hats for tours by Kylie Minogue, Mick Jagger and Marilyn Manson. His philosophy on millinery? 'You have to be a good listener. You have to find out why they are wearing the hat. What they want to achieve. Really, what's going through their mind.'

Jones, who was born in Cheshire, England, studied art before doing a fashion design degree at Saint Martin's School of Art, graduating in 1979. He was one of the original Blitz kids, a coterie of London fashion students who created an undercurrent of post-punk flamboyance. Having interned at couture house Lachasse, where he produced his first millinery concoction of blue crepe de Chine with a silver-sprayed plastic iris,

Jones opened his first shop in Covent Garden within a year of leaving St. Martin's. 'Hats seemed to be the thing that nobody else was doing,' he said, 'I was living from one day to the next. Overnight I had a business.'

His first designer commissions were from Jasper Conran and Zandra Rhodes, but Paris was on the horizon. In 1982 Jones secured a *Tatler* magazine cover and two years later he was hired by Jean Paul Gaultier (p. 249), becoming the first British milliner to create hats for a Paris couturier. He was invited by *Vogue*'s Anna Harvey to provide millinery for Diana, Princess of Wales. He also made hats for singer Boy George. The diversity of clients, projects and inspirations has continued throughout his career.

In 1996 Jones, who had collaborated on Galliano's breakthrough 'Princess Lucretia' collection, was invited to become the official milliner at Christian Dior (p. 73). He has provided hats for a wide variety of advertising campaigns and films. 'Almost all hats are surrealist,' Jones observed. 'I think there are very few hats that aren't.'

Opposite Dior's milliner since 1996, Jones presents a gravity-defying apple green headpiece with side-sweeping foliage. Autumn/Winter 2007.

Stephen Jones

1920

1930

1940

1950

1957 Born in Cheshire, England

1960

1970

1975 Studies at High Wycombe College of Art
1976 Studies fashion at Saint Martin's School of Art

1980 Opens first millinery store in basement of PX in London's Covent Garden

1984 Relocates flagship store to Soho; makes Paris debut with hats for Jean Paul Gaultier and Thierry Mugler

1990

1996 Invited by John Galliano to be milliner at Christian Dior

2000

2009 Creates hats for Audrey Tautou in Coco Avant Chanel; stages major exhibition at V&A
2010 Awarded an OBE

2013 Curates 'hatOLOGY', a Milanese exhibition dedicated to the wardrobe of his client Anna Piaggi

'I don't understand why everyone calls my style destroy. When I recut clothes, old or new, it's to transform them.'

Martin Margiela

b. 1957

BELGIUM

The name Martin Margiela is surrounded by an aura of elusiveness. Enigmatic, anonymous and averse to giving any kind of interview (so much so that we could not find a portrait to show above), Margiela is known in person to few in fashion's inner circle. His private life – in a way that has drawn parallels with Greta Garbo – is shrouded in mystery.

Part of the Antwerp contingent that included Helmut Lang (p. 253), Dries Van Noten (p. 265) and Ann Demeulemeester, Margiela is known for his experimentalism and avant-garde approach. He has more in common with punk than any other youth movement but more for its rebellious nature than visible points of reference. 'I'm interested in the entire culture of fashion,' he said, 'but I'm not interested in taking one moment of history and copying it.' When the press dubbed his breakthrough collection in 1989 'Destroy' he did not understand it. Ripped T-shirts had shades of the Sex Pistols' do-it-yourself philosophy, but Margiela preferred the term 'deconstruction'.

The son of a hairdresser, Margiela was born in Belgium and at 18 went to study at the Royal Academy of Fine Arts in Antwerp. He moved to Paris in 1984 and was hired by Jean Paul Gaultier (p. 249) when they met at a student competition. Within four years Margiela, with the encouragement of Gaultier – who later said, 'I already knew he was good, but I didn't realize to what extent' – had established his own house and presented his first collection in a Paris parking lot. The deconstructed look, featuring torn and ripped fabrication, was dubbed 'La Nouvelle Vague' by *Vogue*, with the magazine reporting: 'For all his wild style, destroy master Margiela knows how to cut clothes, and he takes his craft seriously, shirking the moniker with which he's been tagged.'

Believing there were far too many clothes in the world that were not worn, Margiela was an originator of what would later be termed 'upcycling', renewing old garments and creating looks from existing ideas. In 1993 Margiela reworked his classic pieces from the previous five years, dyeing them in grey and staging the show in an abandoned supermarket, stating: 'There's nothing new.' Professing that authenticity was integral to his design signature, he declined to hire professional models for his boutique presentations and preferred, instead, to show his clothes on women who resembled his real customers.

In what was regarded as an unexpected appointment, Margiela was invited to be womenswear director at Hermès (p. 9). He took up the position in 1997 and stunned the press at his debut with the low-key normality of the presentation. He was still heading the Maison Martin Margiela, and in October 1998 expanded the line to include menswear. Two years later he opened his first store in Tokyo.

Diesel bought majority share in MMM in 2002. By the time Margiela had left his company, in 2009, the fashion vocabulary he had invented had influenced a new generation. John Galliano (p. 272) is now creative director of the house.

Opposite Hugely influential in his approach to deconstruction, Margiela takes inspiration from a tailor's mannequin for this sleeveless jacket. Spring/Summer 1997.

1920

1930

1940

1950

1957 Born in Genk, Belgium

1960

1970

1979 Graduates from the Royal Academy of Fine Arts at Antwerp
Moves to Paris and assists Jean Paul Gaultier

1984 Establishes own label and redefines grunge with deconstruction, recycling and raw finishes

1988 Becomes Womenswear Director of Hermès

1990

1997 Launches first menswear collection

1998 Maison Martin Margiela becomes a public company with Renzo Rosso, Diesel group owner, acquiring the majority stake

2000

2002 Retrospective in Antwerp

2008 Resigns in October

2009 John Galliano announced as the forthcoming creative director of Maison Martin Margiela

2014

Above Spearheading the recycling revolution, Margiela constructed this halterneck top from vintage kid gloves layered together. 2001.

Opposite Margiela is famous for taking found objects and transforming them into wearables. This belt jacket is the epitome of upcycling. 2006.

'I'm inspired by things
I don't like. I prefer things
which are surprising.'

Dries Van Noten

b. 1958

BELGIUM

A keen gardener who relishes the complexities of running a business as much as creating a new collection, Dries Van Noten has said: 'Doing only the creative part of the job would be boring. What's the point in designing something if afterwards you don't know if it's sold?' His pragmatic, straightforward attitude is indicative of the area where he was born. A member of the avant-garde 'Antwerp Six', Dries Van Noten is known for his sensitive colour palette, ethnic interplay and eccentric use of print. He is a contradiction, pointing out he is more inspired by things he does not like than by the predictability of prettiness. Quiet but outspoken, distinctive but low-key: 'I don't really want to make clothes that shout,' he says by way of explanation.

Unlike his contemporary Ann Demeulemeester, Van Noten is susceptible to decoration, sumptuous fabrication and historic influences. In a Van Noten presentation, traditional and futuristic cloths combine – often in a single eloquent proportion. His philosophy revolves around the clashing of colour, mixing of print and infusion of embroidery. 'I want to tell stories with fabrics, colour and shape,' he says. The Van Noten headquarters are equally eclectic – a distinctive, triangular, five-storey former warehouse in Antwerp that once housed precious fine art is now furnished with Van Noten's collection of antiques.

Van Noten's grandfather was a tailor, his father the founder of Belgium's first designer destination store who provided him with an entrance to the industry. Van Noten studied at the Royal Academy of Fine Arts in Antwerp, financing himself by doing stints of freelance designing. Noting the extremes in that era of fashion – from the distressed look of Comme des Garçons (see Rei Kawakubo, p. 189) to the power shoulders at Claude Montana (p. 233) – Van Noten realized that although he would ultimately show in Paris, his immediate future was in Antwerp. The first sighting of Van Noten's style was as part of the Antwerp Six, who displayed their wares at the London Designer Collections in 1986. Van Noten's 1993 show, in the Hotel George V in Paris, was a delicate display of floral prints and Asian influences. His inspiration came from diverse sources: antique etchings, tropical jungles, Balenciaga silhouettes (p. 53). Of the people who have inspired him most, he names Coco Chanel (p. 41), Christian Dior (p. 73), photographer Cecil Beaton and painters Francis Bacon and Victor Vasarely.

Womenswear apart, Van Noten is also renowned for his menswear, opening his first men's store a stone's throw from his women's boutique on Paris's Left Bank. Fiercely independent, serving as both creative director and chief executive of his company, Van Noten goes against the grain: 'I think there is too much fashion in the world,' he told the *Wall Street Journal* in 2011. 'There is always another collection launch, cruise, resort, accessories, and on and on, and that's a pity.'

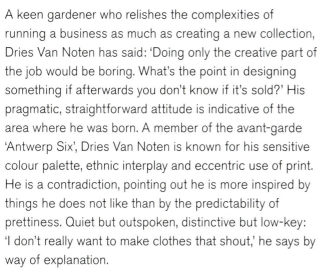

Opposite Folklore was a continual source of inspiration for Van Noten. Here he pairs a layered skirt with collared Nehru jacket, 2002.

Above A number of ethnic influences can be seen in this bohemian interplay of transparency and pattern. 2002.

Opposite top Romantic florals and sensitive colours are applied to menswear. 2005.

Opposite bottom On display here, the perennial Van Noten signature of precisely placing floral embroidery as a focal point. 2009.

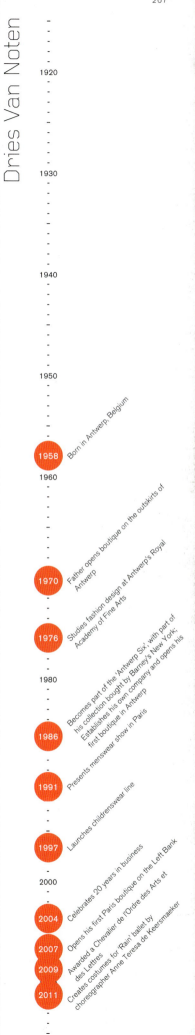

Dries Van Noten

1920

1930

1940

1950

1958 Born in Antwerp, Belgium

1960

1970 Father opens boutique on the outskirts of Antwerp

Studies fashion design at Antwerp's Royal Academy of Fine Arts

1976 Becomes part of the 'Antwerp Six', with part of his collection bought by Barney's New York; Establishes his own company and opens his first boutique in Antwerp

1980

1986 Presents menswear show in Paris

1991 Launches childrenswear line

1997 Celebrates 20 years in business

2000

2004 Opens his first Paris boutique on the Left Bank

2007 Awarded a Chevalier de l'Ordre des Arts et des Lettres

2009 Creates costumes for 'Rain' ballet by choreographer Anne Teresa de Keersmaeker

2011

'It is not necessary to be too avant garde, because you risk not being understood.'

Dolce & Gabbana

Domenico Dolce b. 1958

Stefano Gabbana b. 1962

ITALY

Based on a potent mix of Sicilian sexuality and Milanese imagination, Dolce & Gabbana brought a new brand of Italian dressing to the international arena. 'We looked at our heritage, our beginning, all the elements of our history and made them modern,' they say. 'We built our fashion around three fundamental concepts: Sicily, tailoring and tradition.' Edgy, sultry, sexy, voluptuous, the typical Dolce & Gabbana woman evokes shades of Sophia Loren and the inherent mystique of a Visconti movie. The finer details are fringing, translucency, lace, corsetry – and lots of black. The designers pinpoint a simple black bra as the sexiest item of women's clothing, clarifying that 'it's all about attitude'.

Domenico Dolce and Stefano Gabbana met in a Milanese nightclub in 1980. Dolce had studied fashion, but Gabbana was intending to become a graphic designer. 'We're polar opposites,' Dolce told *Vanity Fair*, 'but we find a centre.' Initially they worked as a freelance partnership, consulting for big brands across Italy. Intent on starting their own label, they produced a small collection, holding shows wherever they could. 'We made absurd presentations, almost insane. Someone really should have calmed us down,' recalled Gabbana, possibly remembering the time they staged a show in a fast-food restaurant. Having the courage of their convictions, however, paid off. In 1985 they were invited by the organizers of Milan Fashion Week to take part in a talent showcase. Working day and night, Dolce and Gabbana opened an office in the Corso di Porta Ticinese. Their only possessions were 'a sewing machine, a vacuum cleaner and a mannequin'.

After their first collection in 1986, entitled 'Real Women', the company grew slowly but surely. They introduced knitwear, then lingerie and beachwear. In 1990 menswear was added, and in 1992 they entered the bridal market, launched a diffusion line called D&G and created a fragrance entitled Sicily. They were more of a slow burn than an overnight success: 'We went through a lot of small stages and we never had a boom.' When demand for their past collections grew, they created a Dolce & Gabbana Vintage line of reissued pieces, introduced in Autumn 2002. Formerly associated with Isabella Rossellini, Kylie Minogue, Madonna and Angelina Jolie, by 2004 Dolce & Gabbana were appealing to a new breed of soul singers, including Beyoncé and Missy Elliot. In 2011, the pair announced their decision to close the D&G line, preferring to focus on the designer end of their operation. Dolce and Gabbana deal in dreams but essentially their design philosophy is rooted in practicality. They make garments to be worn, not cosseted. 'Clothes have a purpose. This is our motto. Today you need emotion when you buy something. You have to love it.'

Opposite The luxurious Sicilian widow look elevated to the level of Parisian haute couture in Dolce & Gabbana's 'Alta Moda' collection, fittingly shown in Sicily. July 2012.

Left Androgyny occasionally makes an appearance, here modelled by Linda Evangelista in a zebra print jacket, trilby and masculine trousers. 1994.

Below A typical celebration of female curves and unashamed sensuality, which often takes underwear as a starting point. 1991.

Opposite Scarlett Johansson films Dolce & Gabbana's commercial for their perfume 'The One' in New York, 2013, directed by Martin Scorsese and co-starring Matthew McConaughey.

Dolce & Gabbana

1920

1930

1940

1950

1958 Domenico Dolce born in Sicily

1960

1962 Stefano Gabbana born in Milan, Italy

1970

1980 Dolce and Gabbana meet in a Milan nightclub

1985 Shown as part of Young Talents Showcase at the invitation of Camera Nazionale della Moda Italiana

1990 Launch of menswear collection; consult for Complice

1993 Commissioned to make stage outfits for Madonna's Girlie Show tour

1994 Flagship store opens on Via della Spiga, Milan; first D&G show presentation

2001 D&G Junior launched

2010 D&G line closed

2011

'Reality is so overrated.'

John Galliano

b. 1960

GIBRALTAR

In the same year (2001) that John Galliano was honoured with a CBE by Queen Elizabeth, American *Vogue* noted matter-of-factly, 'Galliano says his maverick designs are at least 10 per cent madness.' Theatrical, wayward, larger-than-life, Galliano was in pole position at Christian Dior (p. 73) for 14 years. During that time he retained the essence of Dior – sublime structure, unparalleled sense of proportion, technical elegance – and added an extravagance that became unmistakably Galliano. Taking a bow at the end of every collection – couture or ready-to-wear – he would dress in keeping with the season's theme, be it a swashbuckling soldier or a beautifully turned-out farmer complete with flat cap, rake and straw.

Galliano spent his early years in Gibraltar, moving to London with his family when he was 6 years old. As a teenager frequenting such legendary nightclubs as the Blitz and Leigh Bowery's Taboo, during the day Galliano studied painting and drawing at Saint Martin's School of Art. By his final year, he had decided to defect to fashion design. It was here, and in the vaults of London's Victoria and Albert Museum, that his romanticism and historical reference points became a preoccupation. Closing the show in his final year, his graduate presentation was picked up by the *Times*, which reported in 1984: 'John Galliano wound up the Saint Martin's show in (almost) justifiably grandiose style with his androgynous and romantic vision of the Napoleonic era.'

Although he secured a first-class degree and was feted early in his career, Galliano struggled to be commercially viable. In October 1993 he bought a bolt of black satin and threw a wild card, relocating his show to the Hotel Particulier in Paris and persuading a handful of supermodels to don his creations. The conclusion was rapturous applause and positive repercussions, which led him to take the reins two years later at Givenchy (p. 117) and then at Christian Dior.

Coinciding with Dior's fiftieth anniversary in 1997, Galliano's first collection for that couture house took place at the Grand Hotel, Paris. It was the opening gambit that set the scene for more than a decade of phenomenal success. Galliano's incredible creative output enabled him not only to design Dior's seasonal fashion collections but also to oversee accessories, fine jewellery, perfume, makeup and eyewear, in addition to retaining his own label, the John Galliano line.

In March 2011 he suffered a public breakdown and was unceremoniously dismissed by Dior. After being thrown a lifeline by Oscar de la Renta, who offered him a job two years later, Galliano has now taken the post of creative director at Maison Martin Margiela (p. 260).

Opposite Incredible imagination and exquisite cutting techniques come together in this Dior origami evening dress by Galliano. Spring/Summer 2007.

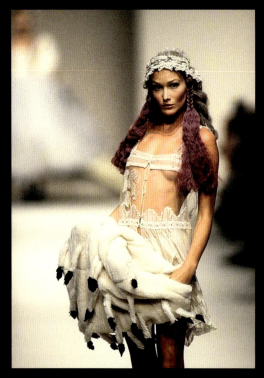

Above left Carla Bruni poses as Princess Lucretia, a fictional character, in Galliano's Spring/Summer 1994 show.

Above right Galliano's graduate show entitled 'Les Incroyables' showed early maverick tendencies. 1984.

Left Hourglass jacket, secured at the waist with double pearl button edging and tippet hem. Spring/Summer 1994.

Opposite Early in Galliano's tenure at Christian Dior, Helena Christensen models a jacquard jacket which leaves little to the imagination. 1997.

John Galliano

1920

1930

1940

1950

1960 Born in Gibraltar

1970

1980

1988 Graduates from Central Saint Martins with first class honours

1990

Appointed designer at Givenchy – the first British designer to lead a French couture house

1995 Moves to Christian Dior
1996

2001 Awarded an OBE

Suspended from Dior over allegations of anti-semitism

2011 Announced as new creative director of Maison Martin Margiela

2014

'Dressing well is a form
of good manners.'

Tom Ford

b. 1961

UNITED STATES

It could be argued that the debonair Tom Ford is a product of his time. Supremely confident, articulate, elegant and astute, Ford has become the benchmark for no-holds-barred success in the fashion industry. The seemingly effortless manner in which he progressed from part-time Hollywood actor to director of one of the world's most luxurious Parisian fashion powerhouses has left both the financiers and his fellow designers in awe. Ford's rebranding and reinvigoration of the Gucci brand (p. 37) has entered the annals of business folklore: in less than a decade, he transformed a traditional symbol into a total phenomenon. Not only did Ford redirect the fashion line, but in one fell swoop he attracted a new coterie of international customers.

While studying at New York University, Ford already had the ability to capture the zeitgeist. His attraction to glamour triggered by an invitation to the nightclub Studio 54 by Andy Warhol, in 1980 Ford dropped out of college after only a year and headed to California. He returned to New York in 1982 to study architecture but eventually defected to fashion. He was employed by Seventh Avenue designer Cathy Hardwick as an assistant and after two years had been offered the position of design director at Perry Ellis. By 1990, Ford was in Milan working for Dawn Mello, then Gucci's creative director. He had overall responsibility for designing the womenswear, menswear and accessory lines, and on Mello's return to New York, Ford was awarded the coveted position. As creative director of Gucci, Ford was given free rein to sell his brand of sartorial sexuality to the fashion-buying public. The positive response was unanimous. Inevitably, celebrity endorsement followed,

with the press picking up on the newly hot label. 'Someone asked Madonna on camera what she was wearing and she said "Gucci, Gucci, Gucci". That was really the beginning,' Ford would later recall.

By the millennium, Ford was spreading his wings. He was now designing the Yves Saint Laurent (p. 165) ready-to-wear collection as well as directing advertising campaigns. Controversy became part of the package and a tool that Ford used to full effect. In 2004 he showed his final Gucci collection and displayed his chameleon-like quality when he signed a licensing deal for fragrances and cosmetics with Estée Lauder. Ford was by now the CEO of his own brand: Tom Ford International.

His break from fashion was short-lived and within 12 months Ford was producing luxury menswear under his own label, followed by the launch of a Manhattan flagship store and plans for global expansion. He was named Menswear Designer of the Year by the Council of Fashion Designers of America in 2008.

Opposite In his final Gucci show, Tom Ford mingled fox fur with silk organza and sequin to devastating effect. Autumn/Winter 2004.

Opposite Referencing sportswear, swimwear and bias cutting, this Gucci dress has all the Ford hallmarks. Autumn/Winter 2004.

Top A curvaceous fur-panelled bolero forms the upper part of a tailored jacket. Autumn/Winter 2004.

Above Ford's version of Yves Saint Laurent kept the crucial components but updated them for a younger clientele. Autumn/Winter 2000.

Tom Ford

1920

1930

1940

1950

1961 Born in Austin, Texas, USA

1970 Family moves to Santa Fe, New Mexico

1972 Studies Art History at New York University, leaving after a year to study at Parsons New School of Design

1979 Starts working for Cathy Hardwick

1980

1986 Starts working for Perry Ellis

1988 Hired as womenswear designer for Gucci by Dawn Mello; promoted 4 years later to Creative
1990 Director

2000 Named Womenswear Designer of the Year by CFDA and Best Fashion Designer at Time magazine

2003 Leaves Gucci
2004 Opens his own film production company
2005

2009 Makes directorial debut with his film A Single Man
2010

'Sometimes I cannot achieve what I really want to do in just one collection. There are certain things I have been working on for three years.'

Junya Watanabe

b. 1961

JAPAN

He has been called 'the most elusive designer in the world', responsible for making 'obscure objects of desire'. As a producer of esoteric outfits, Watanabe has commented: 'I don't expect everyone to understand my work.' A relentless experimentalist who resolutely stands outside the mainstream fashion firmament, he has carved his niche in conceptual thinking and prefers to present rather than explain: 'You can interpret my work as you wish.'

As a protégé of Rei Kawakubo (p. 189), Watanabe began his career as a pattern cutter at Comme des Garçons. Within eight years he had his own label, financially backed by Kawakubo. His mentor has had a distinctly hands-off approach, avoiding any form of artistic intervention.

Immediately after graduation in 1984, Watanabe joined the company that was to become his creative catalyst: Comme des Garçons. His talent for merging ingenious cutting with inventive fabrication not only fitted in perfectly with the company philosophy but was spotted almost immediately. By 1987 Watanabe was promoted to the position of design director for Comme des Garçons Tricot, the company's knitwear line. Stunning the fashion fraternity with his debut collection, Watanabe gave credit not to his formal education but to his unique work experience. Fashion school, he said, simply taught him 'how to use a needle and thread and a sewing machine. Everything else I learned at Comme des Garçons.'

The Watanabe signature – conceptual cutting, surprising seaming, unusual fabrication – was paired with a deconstructive approach to proportion and an instinct to completely ignore international seasonal trends. He specialized in pleating, folding and padding, but also in redefining preconceived ideas about fashion.

Where Watanabe womenswear is relentlessly experimental and pushes the acceptable face of female attire to extremes, his menswear is more rooted in tradition. A typical Watanabe men's jacket – a knitted Fair Isle body with leather sleeves – puts a new twist on a classic technique.

The versatility of Watanabe's approach is universally acknowledged. He has collaborated with Loewe, producing a capsule range of clothing and accessories for both men and women, and has made a futuristic collection of athletic wear for Puma. But it is his pairing with iconic Western brands for menswear that has shown Watanabe's distinctive style to its best advantage: down jackets for outerwear specialists Duvetica, training shoes for New Balance, patchwork blazers for Brooks Brothers, a reconstructed polo shirt for Lacoste and deconstructed jeans for Levi Strauss. 'It's important for me to consider where you wear the clothes and what purpose they serve,' he says.

Opposite Watanabe shows off a water-repellent hat, synthetic pleated shrug and shift under artificial rain. Spring/Summer 2000.

The basic idea of a conventional padded
jacket is here turned into an extraordinary
floor-length, funnel-necked coat.
Autumn/Winter 2009.

Above Surreal bandaged heads and bodies
dressed in various weights of experimentally
cut jersey paraded the catwalk in
Autumn/Winter 2008.

Opposite Dubbed 'extreme beauty', this
magnified ruffle dress is handstitched
polyester organza, from the 'Techno
Couture' collection, Autumn/Winter 2000.

Junya Watanabe

1920

1930

1940

1950

1961 Born in Fukushima, Japan

1970

1980

1984 Graduates from Bunka Fashion College, Tokyo

Initially employed as an apprentice pattern maker, Watanabe is appointed Design Director of Comme des Garçons Tricot, the knitwear division

1987 Backed by his mentor Rei Kawakubo, Watanabe launches his own label Junya Watanabe, Comme des Garçons and presents in Paris the following year

1990

1992 Named by *Vogue* as one to watch

Launches menswear collection inspired by American sports and workwear

2000
2001 Designs capsule collection of All Star Sneakers for Converse

2007 Co-designs collection with Puma

Collaborates with Loewe on capsule collection

2010

2012
2013
2014 Invited to rework Levi's classic 508 design, customized in cotton denim

'Life is a fashion show.
The world is your runway.'

Marc Jacobs

b. 1963

UNITED STATES

The multitalented Marc Jacobs has a rare chameleon-like quality. With the capacity to make the transition from directing an all-American label to designing an A-list Parisian luxury brand, Jacobs still retains the persona of an enfant terrible. 'It's quite nice to see that I didn't have to change who I was to reach two very different types of people,' he said. Looking at least a decade younger than his age, Jacobs has the reputation of being a party animal, but he is also a disciplinarian. Adhering to a strict exercise and diet regime, according to the *New Yorker*, 'He has made his home a museum and his body a work of art beautiful enough to reside there'.

Jacobs's father died when he was seven, and he was raised by his paternal grandmother in an apartment near Central Park West. At 13 he applied to work at the hip New York boutique Charivari and by 17 he was travelling to Paris to attend a summer course courtesy of Parsons School of Design. On the advice of designer Perry Ellis – whom Jacobs had met while working at Charivari – he enrolled at Parsons. At the age of 24, in 1984, Jacobs was named Parsons Design Student of the Year for his capsule collection of Op Art sweaters. Around that time, Jacobs met an executive called Robert Duffy, who was to become his business partner and a significant figure in his life. The sweaters were put into production and sold at Charivari. By November he was making his debut for Sketchbook with a sportswear range he described as 'a bit of Mozart and Prince's trashy sex appeal'. The *New York Times* cited him as a name to watch and *Vogue* listed him as one of seven designers who were creating 'A New Wave'.

Jacobs's rise was nothing less than meteoric. In 1987 he became the youngest designer ever to receive the CFDA's Perry Ellis Award for Fashion Talent, the following year presenting his first collection for the house. Everything was going well until, in 1992, Jacobs decided to make Perry Ellis less Seventh Avenue and more street, explaining: 'Grunge is a hipped romantic version of punk.' Jacobs was fired for his downmarket presentation, which divided public opinion. The departure, however, had positive repercussions. He was offered the newly created position of artistic director of Louis Vuitton in 1997 and within a decade, had quadrupled the business. Merging popular culture with aspirational luxury, Jacobs instigated collaborations with graffiti artist Stephen Sprouse and Japanese avant-garde artist Yayoi Kusama.

In 2013 he presented his last Louis Vuitton show, vowing to focus on the Marc Jacobs brand. 'I love frogs,' he told the *New Yorker*. 'This sort of fairy-tale frog that became a prince, and the chameleon who changes colors with his environment.'

Opposite On his exit from Louis Vuitton, Jacobs sent model Edie Campbell out first wearing a Stephen Sprouse flesh-coloured bodysuit and feather headdress. Spring/Summer 2014.

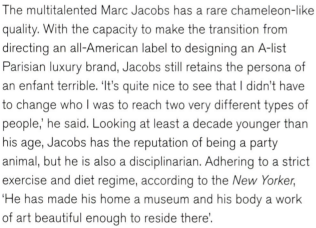

Opposite A deeply plunging, sleeveless polka-dot dress with a triple layered skirt, edged in contrast piping. Resort 2011.

Above This controversial collection earned Jacobs the title 'The Guru of Grunge' in *Women's Wear Daily*. Jacobs's 'homeless chic' show for Perry Ellis, first shown in 1992 for Spring/ Summer 1993.

1920

1930

1940

1950

1960

1963 Born in New York, USA

1970

1978 Works at hip New York boutique Charivari

Wins three awards, including Design Student of the Year at Parsons School of Design

1981 Youngest recipient of Perry Ellis Fashion Talent

1987 First collection for Perry Ellis

1989 Shows infamous grunge collection

1992 Appointed creative director of Louis Vuitton and designs the house's first ready-to-wear line

1997 Introduces his secondary line, Marc by Marc Jacobs

Wins CFDA Accessory Designer of the Year award

2001

2003 Exhibition of his work held at Musée des Arts Décoratifs, Paris

2010

2012
2013 Announces his departure from Louis Vuitton to focus on his own label

'Hats are about emotion. It's all about how it makes you feel.'

Philip Treacy

b. 1967

REPUBLIC OF IRELAND

'She invented me. She introduced me to everything I know,' said hat designer Philip Treacy of his muse, soulmate and ardent supporter, the late Isabella Blow. Treacy was spotted by Blow as a student at London's Royal College of Art, and she not only modelled his hats in his graduation show but installed him in her Belgravia basement and commissioned him to make an ornate gold lace wimple for her forthcoming wedding. It was an entrance that catapulted the unknown Irishman to fashion wonderland. Treacy believes it is the wearer, not the hat, that is the most important element: 'A person carries off the hat,' he maintains, adding, 'I like hats that make the heart beat faster.'

Born in the west of Ireland, Treacy moved to Dublin in 1985 to study fashion. Initially he made hats as 'a hobby', but when he undertook a six-week internship at Stephen Jones his interest in millinery became a serious preoccupation. During his MA at the Royal College of Art in 1988, Treacy specialized in hat-making, entering and winning a Harrods competition to create a collection. In 1989 Treacy took some of his hats to show *Tatler*'s fashion director, Michael Roberts, and style editor, Isabella Blow. The meeting changed the course of his career and paved the way for his success, as Blow continued to wear his hats throughout her life. Describing their connection, he said: 'It was more than just a collaboration, it was a kind of romance, a love affair about hats.' The relationship between Blow and Treacy was embodied in an exhibition in 2002 entitled 'When Philip

Met Isabella' at London's Design Museum. It included a black satin and feather hat in the shape of a galleon, which would later adorn Blow's coffin at her funeral.

Introduced to Karl Lagerfeld (p. 157) via Blow, at 23 years old Treacy found himself designing a twisted birdcage for Chanel (p. 41). He staged his first catwalk show in 1993, with a line-up of supermodels showing his collection of all-black hats. Of all his collaborations, those with Alexander McQueen (p. 297) were his favourite. 'He would say, "I want the hats to look like they've been found on a futuristic rubbish dump,"' recalled Treacy.

Treacy's talent lies in his diverse repertoire – a telephone hat for Lady Gaga, a wheat-sheaf tiara for Camilla Parker Bowles, feathers spelling the word 'H-A-T' for Erin O'Connor. But Treacy has an aversion to the term 'milliner'. 'It's not a true reflection of what I do,' he says. 'It's an eighteenth-century term, when a milliner was someone who decorated dresses à la Marie-Antoinette. I believe that I am a hat designer, not a milliner.'

Opposite This spectacular, intricate galleon hat with vintage feathered sails, designed in 1994, ultimately adorned the coffin of Treacy's mentor, Isabella Blow, at her funeral in May 2007.

Above Vibrant orange plumes, found by Treacy in California, are here strategically placed to frame the face and secured on a silk satin base. 1996.

Left Taking the front row position at Treacy's London Fashion Week show in September 2012, the pop artist Lady Gaga wears a space-age helmet adorned in silk flowers.

Opposite The outlandish, curvaceous straw hat entitled 'Madonna Rides Again', previously worn by Isabella Blow's sister-in-law at her wedding.

Philip Treacy

Born in County Galway, West Ireland

1920   1930   1940   1950   1960   **1967** 1970

Moves to Dublin to study fashion at National
College of Art and Design

Graduates from the Royal College of Art,
having met Isabella Blow and commissioned to
make the headpiece for her wedding

First solo show

Stages the first ever couture show devoted
solely to hats

'When Philip Met Isabella' exhibition shown at
the Design Museum, London

Awarded an OBE

One of 6 contemporary designers to feature on
a set of Irish postage stamps

1985　1990　1993　2000　'02　2007　2010

'Fashion somehow, for me, is purely and happily irrational.'

Hedi Slimane

b. 1968

FRANCE

Such is the seductive quality of a Hedi Slimane suit that Karl Lagerfeld (p. 157) underwent a serious diet to be able to wear one. 'I wanted to be a perfect coathanger for slim-fitting clothes,' Lagerfeld said in 2001, 'I suddenly wanted to wear clothes designed by Hedi Slimane.' The Parisian designer with an air of melancholy, who made his name redrawing a new proportion of the slimline man's suit, credited the inspiration to 'the whole idea of masculinity that could be applied to creative fields'. Pierre Bergé, who installed Slimane to direct Yves Saint Laurent menswear, was unprepared for the impact Slimane would create. 'I had six months to think about what I wanted to do,' said Slimane.

Christened the 'Prince of Darkness' by *GQ*, Slimane's own striking appearance and aura of cool attracted a new generation of customers to Yves Saint Laurent. His image was underlined by a coterie of admirers who included Mick Jagger, bands such as Franz Ferdinand, the Libertines and the Kills, and Slimane's hero, David Bowie.

Born to an Italian mother and Tunisian father, Slimane was a keen photographer as a boy and was technically proficient in the darkroom. He studied history of art at the École du Louvre in Paris. In the early 1990s Slimane assisted menswear designer José Lévy, before working with fashion consultant Jean-Jacques Picard on an exhibition celebrating the centenary of the Louis Vuitton monogram. The project entailed the coordination of seven fashion designers – Helmut Lang (p. 253), Sybilla, Azzedine Alaïa (p. 181), Manolo Blahnik, Isaac Mizrahi, Romeo Gigli and Vivienne Westwood (p. 185). Spotted by Bergé, Slimane was the unexpected appointment to head the Saint Laurent menswear collection in 1996. The praise was effusive. 'Under the sharp eye and scissors of the design director, Hedi Slimane, Saint Laurent's classics have turned hip,' reported the *International Herald Tribune*.

When the label was acquired by the Gucci Group in 1999 and Slimane transferred to Christian Dior (p. 73), his first collection in January 2001, entitled 'Solitaire', sealed his growing reputation as a meticulous arbiter of taste; Yves Saint Laurent himself led a standing ovation. With an aesthete's eye and obsessive work ethic, Slimane not only directed the collection but was also involved in the lighting, music and model casting – often eschewing professional models in favour of naturally stylish people he saw in the street.

Lured back to Yves Saint Laurent in 2012, though still based in Los Angeles, Slimane designed the womenswear collection in the autumn of that year, giving a nod to 1970s bohemia. The reviews were mixed but sales remained buoyant.

Opposite A twenty-first-century translation of the traditional biker jacket, worn with nothing except a pair of low-slung trousers. 2014.

Above Referencing Yves Saint Laurent's historic and controversial nod to nudity, Slimane's 2013 catwalk featured a sheer blouse, sleek tailoring and slimline leather tie.

Opposite A modern take on bohemia with floor-sweeping cape, floppy hat, skinny, shiny trousers and chiffon oversized bow. 2013.

Hedi Slimane

1920

1930

1940

1950

1960

1968 Born in Paris, France

1970

1980

1984 Studies art history at the École du Louvre and starts to make his own clothes

1989 Hired by José Lévy to help with his menswear collection

1996 Moves to Yves Saint Laurent as assistant but is soon made director of men's ready-to-wear

1999 Leaves Yves Saint Laurent

2001 First Dior Homme collection receives rave reviews

2007 Resigns from Dior and leaves for Los Angeles

2011 Curates exhibition of his own photographs

2012 Returns to Yves Saint Laurent

2014 Largest YSL flagship store designed by Slimane opens on Rodeo Drive, Los Angeles

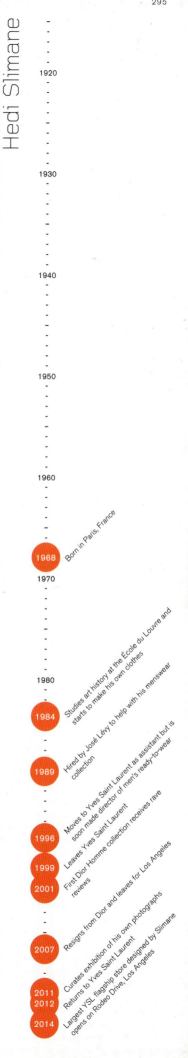

'I know I'm provocative.
You don't have to like it, but
you have to acknowledge it.'

Alexander McQueen

1969–2010

UNITED KINGDOM

With an antenna for impact and a talent to shock, Alexander McQueen made fashion history via his fearless attitude and aptitude for causing a stir. He created not only waves with his clothes but controversy with his shows. Accused variously of being a misogynist and sadomasochist, he also riled the animal rights activists and caused the Hell's Angels to file a lawsuit. Throughout his short but spectacular reign as Britain's enfant terrible, McQueen straddled the worlds of high fashion and high drama. 'People find my things sometimes aggressive,' he told *W* magazine in 2002, 'but I don't see it as aggressive. I see it as romantic, dealing with a dark side of a personality.'

Son of a London taxi driver, and one of six children, McQueen enjoyed a meteoric rise – from Central Saint Martins hopeful to international powerhouse – which was made possible by a fortuitous meeting with British *Vogue*'s star-spotter, Isabella Blow. It was she who choreographed the initial stages of his career, wearing his graduate MA collection in November 1992 on the pages of British *Vogue*, garnering contacts, and cajoling him into changing his name from Lee to the more aristocratic-sounding Alexander (his middle name). With previous training on Savile Row and experience in pattern cutting with Koji Tatsuno and Romeo Gigli, McQueen already understood the complexities of tailoring long before he embarked on a career in fashion design.

McQueen's most memorable and long-lasting invention was the 'bumster' trouser shape – launched in Spring/Summer 1995 – exposing the upper part of the posterior. With collection titles ranging from 'Jack the Ripper Stalks his Victims' to 'Highland Rape' and reams of media coverage, the foundations were laid for the bad boy of British fashion to make his international entrance. At the age of 27, McQueen secured the position of chief designer at Givenchy (p. 117), the Parisian couture house regarded as an emblem of restraint, but his first collection was universally panned and the tenure was relatively short-lived. Brokered again by Blow, the Gucci Group agreed to finance McQueen's own label.

McQueen became increasingly adventurous in his approach to fashion, featuring an amputee on the catwalk in 1998 and a large, naked woman wearing a gas mask in a moth-filled glass cage in 2000.

The year after his suicide in 2010, McQueen's legacy was showcased in an exhibition entitled 'Savage Beauty' at the Metropolitan Museum of Art, New York. Featuring extreme silhouettes, images of the crucifixion and corsetry resembling a ribcage, it was a testament to his experimental cutting techniques and abiding passions. 'Beauty can come from the strangest places,' McQueen was quoted as saying. 'Even the most disgusting places.'

Opposite Mixing the macabre with the seductive, taxidermy with dramatic tension, Hitchcock's 1963 film *The Birds* was a major influence in this 2001 collection, which was staged inside a huge, two-way mirrored box.

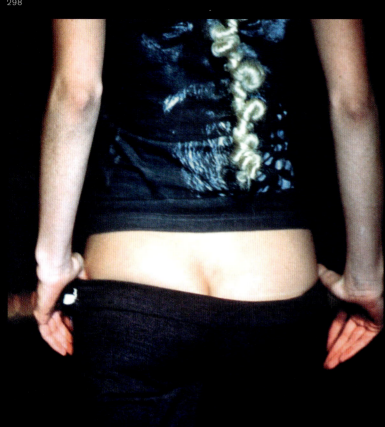

Left McQueen's bumster trouser, cut low on the hip to expose the upper part of the posterior, had a lasting impact on mainstream fashion. 1996.

Below Patron, staunch supporter and industry insider, stylist Isabella Blow sits on the front row next to McQueen's mother Joyce at the Autumn/Winter 2004 show.

Opposite Choreographed to echo religious references to the crucifixion, a strapless boned dress with train is caught in a simulated shower in the June 2004 'Black' show in London.

Alexander McQueen

1920

1930

1940

1950

1960

1969 Born in London, England

1980

1985 Leaves school to take up apprenticeship with
Savile Row tailors Anderson & Sheppard,
then Gieves & Hawkes

1990
1992 Graduates from Central Saint Martins; meets patron
and muse Isabella Blow

Introduces low slung 'bumster' trousers

1995 Named British Designer of the Year by the British
1996 Fashion council; appointed head designer at
Givenchy

Presents final collection for Givenchy

2001 Awarded a CBE; named BFC British Designer
2003 of the Year

His diffusion line, McQ, hits the stores

2006 Designs sportswear and accessories for Puma

2009
2010 Commits suicide

'I think of fashion as an art form as well as an industrial product.'

Hussein Chalayan

b. 1970

CYPRUS

'I work like an artist who happens to use clothes as his medium,' said Hussein Chalayan. 'It took me a long time to admit this.' Known in fashion circles as a thinker, an analyst and an instigator of new ideas, Chalayan is always pushing boundaries. Each collection explores new territory, invariably treading the line between fine art and futuristic fashion. His presentations straddle the worlds of theatrical happening and cultural experience. He is a perfectionist who experiments with a wide variety of media and can switch from directing a film to designing a collection. Collaborations with furniture designers, lighting technicians, technological experts and interactive developers have added a unique dimension to Chalayan's work, to the extent that garments bearing the Hussein Chalayan label are equally at home suspended from a garment rail or on display in a museum. 'I aim to create a new comment on what already exists,' he declared. 'I do play with codes that people are familiar with.'

Cypriot-born Chalayan moved to London with his father in 1982, and on leaving school took a foundation course at Warwickshire School of Arts. A career in fashion beckoned and a place at Central Saint Martins followed, with Chalayan making an indelible impression with his graduate collection, entitled 'The Tangent Flows'. Buried in a garden together with iron filings and featuring fabrication encouraged to decompose, the clothes were then exhumed encrusted with rust. Chalayan's intriguing fashion statement secured a prime spot in the window of Browns fashion boutique on London's South Molton Street. The seed was sown.

Following a brief apprenticeship with Savile Row tailor Timothy Everest, Chalayan decided to go it alone, presenting dresses printed with poetic texts in March 1994, followed by a fully-fledged collection in October at London Fashion Week. Icelandic singer Björk declared herself an admirer and wore his paper jacket on the front cover of her album *Post*, later modelling for his autumn show in 1995. The following year, the first of many exhibitions dedicated to Chalayan's work was mounted in Prague, and global recognition ensued. Constantly struggling with the need to be financially solvent yet protect his artistic integrity, Chalayan took on a series of consultancy appointments including TSE cashmere, Autograph for Marks & Spencer, Asprey, Puma and Swarovski.

Chalayan's heart, however, lay in experimentation rather than commercialization. He screened films at collections, invented mechanized dresses and designed tables that turned into skirts. Hailed by *Vogue* in 2000 as 'the premier intellectual designer of his generation', he was also included that year in *Time* magazine's list of the 100 most influential innovators of the twenty-first century. A decade later, Lady Gaga arrived at the Grammy Awards in a temperature-controlled egg designed by Chalayan. It made headlines around the world. 'I will do whatever feels right,' he said, 'because I don't want to be a slave to someone else's expectations.'

Opposite Elongated organic extensions, based on the concept of speed, flow from the back of an aerodynamic, moulded latex dress from the 'Inertia' collection. Spring/Summer 2009.

Opposite top, left and right Interactive, abstract dress where the skirt flares outwards with the assistance of programmed computer chips. 'One Hundred and Eleven' collection, Spring/ Summer 2007.

Opposite bottom The 'Afterwords' collection, where clothes were disguised as furniture and fibreglass garments were broken with miniature hammers. Autumn/Winter 2000.

Above Conceptual thinking translated into a sartorial jigsaw puzzle of pieces which interact and complement each other in the 'Before Minus Now' show. Spring/Summer 2000.

1920
1930
1940
1950
1960

1970 Born in Nicosia, Cyprus

1978 Studies in England, returning to Cyprus a year later

1980

1989 Studies fashion at Central Saint Martins

1990 Graduation collection displayed by Browns, launching his career

1993 Exhibition of work staged in Prague

1996 Wins Designer of the Year

**1999
2000** Cited in *Time* magazine's 100 most influential innovators of the twenty-first century

2010

'I think in black.'

Gareth Pugh

b. 1981

UNITED KINGDOM

'I have never been a fan of catwalk theatrics,' declared Gareth Pugh, who is known for his gravity-defying dresses, aerodynamic silhouettes and inflatable creations. The designer, who was dubbed 'the Mad Prince of British Fashion' by the *Sunday Times*, has summed up his shows as 'a whole world of otherness' and the process as chaotic. 'Everyone's shows are fraught,' he said, 'but mine seem to be the pinnacle of fraughtness.' Mentored by designer Rick Owens and photographer Nick Knight, Pugh counts fashion icon Daphne Guinness and editor Anna Dello Russo among his fans. His occasionally unnerving style – mixing gimp masks with linear graphics, ghoulish makeup with body armour, moulded hoods with surreal proportions – has met with a mixed reaction. As *Time Out* magazine observed: 'Pugh has the ability to delight and disgust people simultaneously.'

Pugh's childhood was spent taking ballet lessons and his teenage summers assisting in the costume department of the National Youth Theatre; his observation that 'frivolity is important to creativity' seems to belie his inherent work ethic. Born in Sunderland, in northeast England, at 10 years old he was displaying his thespian leanings, playing an owl in the local pantomime. In the same year it was after seeing *The Phantom of the Opera* in London's West End that he realized he wanted to relocate to the capital. Pugh studied sociology in Sunderland, followed by an arts foundation course. He completed a fashion degree at Central Saint Martins, securing a front cover of *Dazed and Confused* magazine with his graduation collection. Following his launch under the Fashion East umbrella in February 2005, the following year Pugh was given sponsorship and made his

debut at London Fashion Week, prompting American *Vogue*'s editor, Anna Wintour, to observe: 'At Gareth Pugh, I see Mugler, Montana and McQueen in the designs. It's fun and eccentric and wonderfully English.'

It was not until August 2007 that Pugh's collection was available for sale to the public and he showed in Paris for the first time. By 2010 he had a retail presence in the Far East, with a small store in Hong Kong situated between Comme des Garçons and Gucci. Pugh, who was one of the first designers to fully embrace the concept of online fashion presentations, fervently believes clothes are a catalyst for change: 'You are transforming yourself from something you are to something you want to be.' During his career he has progressed from having a dozen outfits with nothing for sale to a 350-piece collection, made in Italy and sold globally. 'A lot of what I do has a sense of humour,' he told Nick Knight's Showstudio.com, 'but maybe the audience don't get it so much any more.' He remains the antithesis of the classic fashion brand. 'I don't make things to complement your lifestyle,' he said. 'I do things to make it a bit more interesting.'

Opposite A surreal inflatable statement in black and white, featured in the 'Fashion in Motion' extravaganza at London's Victoria and Albert Museum, 2007.

Muse, mentor and staunch supporter, the impeccably dressed Daphne Guinness wears a Pugh zip shift constructed from horizontal strips. 2011.

Gareth Pugh

1920

1930

1940

1950

1960

1970

1981 Born in Sunderland, England

1990 Begins taking ballet lessons

1995 Internship at the National Youth Theatre in the costume department

2000 Completes art foundation course at City of Sunderland College

2003 Graduates from Central Saint Martins

2005 Presents first collection within the Fashion East initiative

2008 Makes his Paris debut; his work appears in the Metropolitan Museum of Art, New York

2010 Opens first standalone shop in Hong Kong, located between Comme des Garçons and Gucci

Further Reading

Arizzoli-Clémentel, Pierre, et al. *Balenciaga*. (San Sebastian: Editorial Nera, 2011).

Blow, Isabella, Philip Treacy and Hamish Bowles. *Philip Treacy: 'When Philip Met Isabella'* (New York: Assouline, 2002).

Bolton, Andrew, and Harold Koda. *Alexander McQueen: Savage Beauty* (Yale University Press: 2011).

Chalayan, Hussein. *Hussein Chalayan* (New York: Rizzoli International Publications, 2014).

Charles-Roux, Edmonde. *Chanel and her World* (London: Weidenfeld & Nicolson, 1981).

Coleman, Elizabeth, A. *The Genius of Charles James* (Holt, Rinehart and Winston, 1982).

Demornex, Jacqueline. *Vionnet* (London: Thames and Hudson, 1991).

De Osma, Guillermo. *Mariano Fortuny: His Life and Work.* (London: Aurum Press, 1980).

Dior, Christian. *Dior by Dior* (London: Weidenfeld and Nicolson, 1957).

Ferragamo, Salvatore. *Shoemaker of Dreams* (London: George G. Harrap & Co. Ltd, 1957).

Giannini, Frida. *Gucci: The Making Of* (New York: Rizzoli, 2011).

Guillaume, Valerie. *Courrèges Fashion Memoir* (London: Thames and Hudson, 1998).

Hartnell, Norman. *Silver and Gold* (London: Evans Brothers Ltd, 1955).

Howell, Georgina. *In Vogue: Six Decades of Fashion* (London: Allen Lane, 1975).

Hulanicki, Barbara. *From A to Biba* (London: Hutchinson, 1983).

Join-Dieterle, Catherine. *Givenchy: 40 Years of Creation* (Paris: Paris-Musees, 1991).

Jones, Stephen (with contributions by John Galliano, Hamish Bowles, et al). *Stephen Jones & The Accent of Fashion* (ACC Editions: 2010).

Kennedy, Shirley. *Pucci: A Renaissance in Fashion* (New York: Abbeville Press, 1991).

Lacroix, Christian. *Pieces of a Pattern* (London: Thames and Hudson, 1992).

Menkes, Suzy, and Nathalie Bondil. *The Fashion Universe of Jean Paul Gaultier: From the Street to the Stars.* (London: Abrams, 2011).

Merceron, Dean, and Alber Elbaz. *Lanvin* (New York: Rizzoli, 2007).

Moffitt, Peggy, and William Claxton. *The Rudi Gernreich Book* (New York: Rizzoli, 1991).

Morais, Richard. *Pierre Cardin: The Man Who Became A Label* (London: Bantam Press, 1991).

Mouzat, Virginie, and Colombe Pringle. *Roger Vivier* (New York: Rizzoli, 2013).

Mower, Sarah. *Oscar: The Style, Inspiration and Life of Oscar de la Renta* (New York: Assouline, 2002).

Pasols, Paul-Gérard, and Pierre Leonforte. *Louis Vuitton: The Birth of Modern Luxury* (New York: Abrams, 2012).

Pelle, Marie-Paule, and Patrick Mauries. *Valentino: Thirty Years of Magic* (New York: Abbeville Press, 1991).

Poiret, Paul. *My First Fifty Years* (London: V. Gollancz, 1931).

Prada, Miuccia, and Patrizio Bertelli. *Prada* (Milan: Fondazione Prada, 2009).

Quant, Mary. *Quant by Quant* (London: Cassell & Company Ltd, 1966).

Saillard, Olivier. *Madame Grès: Sculptural Fashion* (Belgium: Cannibal/ Hannibal Publishers, 2012).

Schiaparelli, Elsa. *Shocking Life* (London: J. M. Dent & Sons Ltd, 1954).

Steele, Valerie. *Fashion, Italian Style* (New Haven and London: Yale University Press, 2003).

Vercelloni, Isa T., ed. *Missonologia: The World of Missoni* (Milan/New York: Electra/Abbeville Press, 1995).

Versace, Gianni, and Omar Calabrese. *Versace: Signatures* (New York, Abbeville Press, 1993).

Wilcox, Claire. *Vivienne Westwood* (London: V&A Publications, 2004).

Wolcott, James, and Marylou Luther. *Beene by Beene* (New York: The Vendome Press, 2005).

Worth, Jean Philippe. *A Century of Fashion* (Boston: Little Brown and Co., 1928).

Yamamoto, Yohji. *My Dear Bomb* (Antwerp: Ludion, 2010).

Yves Saint Laurent, with introduction by Diana Vreeland (New York: The Metropolitan Museum of Art, 1983).

Index

Picture Credits

8 Donald Honeyman/Condé Nast Publications **10** © Anthea Simms **11L** Roger Viollet/ Rex Features **11TR** © RA/Lebrecht Music & Arts **11BR** © Bettmann/Corbis **12** DEA Picture Library/Getty Images **13** Hulton Archive/Getty Images **14** © Roger-Viollet/TopFoto **15T** © Roger-Viollet/TopFoto **15B** Chicago History Museum/Getty Images **16** Patrick Demarchelier/ Condé Nast Publications **18** Henry Guttmann/ Getty Images **19TL**© Lordprice Collection/Alamy **19BL** catwalking.com **19R** © Rick Piper Photography/Alamy **20** © The Art Archive/Alamy **21** Alinari/Rex Features **22** David Vogue Magazine/Condé Nast Publications **23T** Private Collection/The Stapleton Collection/Bridgeman Images **23B** © Roger-Viollet/TopFoto **24** The Museum of Modern Art, New York/Scala, Florence **25** © Alinari/TopFoto **26** Courtesy Smithsonian Institution **27T** De Agostini Picture Library/Bridgeman Images **27B** LACMA/Art Resource, New York Scala, Florence **28** René Bouët-Willaumez/Condé Nast Publications **29** © Apic/Getty Images **30** George Hoyningen-Huene/Condé Nast Publications **31T** Edward Steichen/Condé Nast Publications **31B** © RA/ Lebrecht Music & Arts **32** Chicago History Museum/Getty Images **33** Everett Collection/ Rex **34L** © RA/Lebrecht Music & Arts **34R** © 2005 Roger-Viollet/Topfoto **35** akg-images/ ullstein bild **36** catwalking.com **37** Thomas Kristich/Getty Images **38T** Karen Radkai/Condé Nast Publications **38B** © The Metropolitan Museum of Art/Art Resource New York/Scala, Florence **39** Elisabetta Catalono/Condé Nast Publications **40** © Chanel/Photo Karl Lagerfeld **41** © Roger-Viollet/TopFoto **42** © Condé Nast/ Vogue France – Photo Sante Forlano **42–43** © Roger-Viollet/TopFoto **44** René Bouët-Willaumez/Condé Nast Publications **45** Popperfoto/Getty Images **46T** © Philadelphia Museum of Art/Corbis **46B** Philadelphia Museum of Art, Pennsylvania, PA, USA/Gift of Mme Elsa Schiaparelli, 1969/Bridgeman Images **47** akg-images/Ullsteinbild **48** Horst P. Horst/ Condé Nast Publications **49** The Granger Collection/Topfoto **50** © RA/Lebrecht Music & Arts **51L** Cecil Beaton/Condé Nast Publications **51R** © Mary Evans Picture Library **52** Frances McLaughlin-Gill/Condé Nast Publications **53** Lipnitzki/Roger Viollet/Getty Images **54–55** Henry Clarke/Condé Nast Publications **55T** Clifford Coffin/Condé Nast Publications **55B** Chicago History Museum/Getty Images **56** Herbert Matter/Condé Nast Publications **57** © David Lees/Corbis **58T** Toscani Archive/Alinari Archives Management, Florence **58B** © Topfoto **59** Courtesy Museo Salvatore Ferragamo, Firenze **60** Photograph by Milton H. Greene/Time & Life Pictures/Getty Images **61** AP/Press Association Images **62T** © Jack Mitchell/Corbis **62B** © The Metropolitan Museum of Art/Art Resource New York/Scala, Florence **63** Bert Stern/Condé Nast Publications **64** © Mary Evans Picture Library 2008 **65** Ward/Associated Newspapers/Rex **66L** © Bettmann/Corbis **66R** V&A Images **67** Popperfoto/Getty Images **68** Rex/Roger-Viollet **69** Bibliotheque des Arts Decoratifs, Paris, France/Archives Charmet/Bridgeman Images **70T** Photo by Hubert Fanthomme/Paris Match via Getty Images **70B** Albin Guillot/Roger Viollet/ Getty Images **71** © Bettmann/Corbis **72** Frances McLaughlin-Gill/Condé Nast Publications **73** Kammerman/Gamma-Rapho via Getty Images **74** Münchner Stadtmuseum, Sammlung Fotografie, Archiv Relang **75T** © The Metropolitan Museum of Art/Art Resource/Scala, Florence **75B** Topham Picturepoint **76** John Rawlings/Condé Nast Publications **77** Parsons School of Design Alumni Association records, New School Archives and Special Collection, The New School, New York, NY **78** Serge Balkin/ Condé Nast Publications **79T** © Genevieve Naylor/Corbis **79B** © The Metropolitan Museum of Art/Art Resource New York/Scala, Florence **80**, **81**, **82–83** Cecil Beaton/Condé Nast Publications **84** ©Topfoto.co.uk **85** © Bettmann/ Corbis **86** Paul Schutzer/Time Life Pictures/ Getty Images **87TL** © DLM - Ledermuseum Offenbach **87TR**, **87B** V&A Images **88** Horst P. Horst/Condé Nast Publications **89** Rex/ Roger-Viollet **90** © Bettmann/Corbis **91T** akg-images/Gerd Hartung **91B** The Art Archive/ Kharbine-Tapabor **92** Horst P. Horst/Condé Nast Publications **93** akg-images/Album **94** Rex/ Snap **95** © Bettmann/Corbis **96** Henry Clarke/ Condé Nast Publications **97** © David Lees/ Corbis **98** Giorgio Lotti/Mondadori Portfolio via Getty Images **99** John Rawlings/Condé Nast Publications **100** Hulton Archive/Getty Images **101** Giuseppe Pino/Mondadori Portfolio via Getty Images **102** © Alessandro Bianchi/Reuters **103** © Topfoto.co.uk **104** © Peter Knapp/Musée Niepce **105** Rex/Roger-Viollet 106 Rex/ Unimedia International **107** Manuel Litran/Paris Match via Getty Images **108** Traina Sal/Condé Nast Publications **109** Rex/c.CSU Archv/Everett **110** © Bettmann/Corbis **111** Courtesy of the FIDM Museum at the Fashion Institute of Design & Merchandising, Los Angeles, CA/Photo Brian Sanderson **112** Camera Press/J.L.Sieff/Queen **113** Russell Mary/Condé Nast Publications **114–115** Bill Ray/Getty Images **116** Rex/ITV **117** akg-images/Gerd Hartung **118** Nat Farbman/The LIFE Picture Collection/Getty Images **119** John Rawlings/Condé Nast Publications **120** © Anthea Simms **121** © Everett Collection Historical/Alamy **122** Chris von Wangenheim/Condé Nast Publications **123T** Lyn Alweis/The Denver Post via Getty Images **123B** Patrick Demarchelier/Condé Nast Publications **124** © National Museums Scotland **125** Rex/Times Newspapers Ltd **126** © National Museums Scotland **127T** © V&A Images/Alamy **127B** © National Museums Scotland **128** © Topfoto **129** Rex/Julien Chatelin **130** Courtesy of Sonia Rykiel. Photo by Graziano Ferrari **131** Courtesy of Sonia Rykiel. Photo by Omnia Diffusion **132** © Denis Piel **133** Traina Sal/ Condé Nast Publications **134** Craig McDean/ Condé Nast Publications **135** © Wally McNamee/Corbis **136** Pittman Dustin/Condé Nast Publications **137** Tony Palmieri/Condé Nast Publications **138** Duane Michals/Condé Nast Publications **139T** Ron Galella/WireImage/Getty Images **139B** Rez/Zuma **140** Rex/Miquel Benitez **141** © Gianni Giansanti/Sygma/Corbis **142** © Julio Donoso/Sygma/Corbis **143** Henry Clarke/Condé Nast Publications **144** © Denis Piel **145** © Sergio Gaudenti/Kipa/Corbis **146** akg-images/E. Mierendorff **147** © Denis Piel **148** catwalking.com **149** Terry O'Neill/Getty Images **150** © Ronald Grant Archive/Topfoto **151** Donato Sardella/Condé Nast Publications **152** PA Archive/Press Association Images **153** Keystone/Getty Images **154** Image Courtesy of The Advertising Archives **155T** © Ullsteinbild/ Topfoto **155B** V&A Images **156** Chris Barham/ Associated News/Rex **157** Rex/Sipa Press **158** © Benoit Tessier/Reuters **159L** © Pierre Vauthey/Sygma/Corbis **159R** Guy Marineau/ Condé Nast Publications **160** Justin de Villeneuve/Hulton Archive/Getty Images **161**, **162** © Topfoto **163** Justin de Villeneuve/Getty Images **164** Francois Gragnon/Paris Match via Getty Images **165** © RDA/Getty Images **166** akg-images/Interfoto **167** Reg Lancaster/Getty Images **168** © Douglas Kirkland/Corbis **169** © Frederic de Lafosse/Sygma/Corbis **170** The Museum of Modern Art, New York/Scala, Florence **171** © Studio Holle-Suppa **172** © Peter Knapp **173** Action Press/Rex **174** catwalking. com **175** Daniel Simon/Gamma/Getty Images **176** Arthur Elgort/Condé Nast Publications **177** Steve Wood/Rex Features **178T** Moviestore Collection/Rex Features **178B** Everett Collection/Rex Features **179** George Crouter/ The Denver Post/Getty Images **180** Sipa Press/ Rex Features **181** © Marianne Haas/Corbis **182–83** Sipa Press/Rex Features **184** Steve Wood/Rex Features **185** Topham Picturepoint **186** David Dagley/Rex **187T** Rex Features **187B**, **188** catwalking.com **189** Iannaccone Thomas/ Condé Nast Publications **190** V&A Images **191T** Frederique Dumoulin/Corbis **191B** Los Angeles County Museum of Art/Art Resource/Scala **192** Courtesy of the Richard Avedon Foundation **193** Jerry Soloway/© Bettmann/Corbis **194** © Fairchild Photo Service/Condé Nast/Corbis **195T** Image courtesy of the Advertising Archives **195B** News (UK) Ltd/Rex **196** Patrick Lichfield/ Condé Nast Publications **197** Ian Tyas/Keystone Features/Getty Images **198** V&A Images **199** Ian Dickson/Redferns/Getty Images **200** © Anthea Simms **201** © Ullsteinbild/Topfoto **202** © Anthea Simms **203T** Art Streiber/Condé Nast Publications **203B** © Ullsteinbild/Topfoto **204** © Norman Parkinson/Sygma/Corbis **205** Central Press/Hulton Archive/Getty Images **206** © Hulton-Deutsch Collection/Corbis **207T** © V&A Images/Alamy **207B** © Apple Corps Ltd **208** Sipa Press/Rex Features **209** © Jérôme Bonnet/Corbis Outline **210T** Mark Large/Daily Mail/Rex **210B** catwalking.com **211** John Bright/Condé Nast Publications **212** © Masayoshi Sukita **213** Photo by Dave M. Benett/ Getty Images **214** Bridgeman Images **215T** Evening Standard/Getty Images **215B** Rose Hartman/Wireimage/Getty Images **216** © Luke MacGregor/Reuters/Corbis **217** Imaginechina/ Rex Features **218L** Bruno Vincent/Getty Images **218R** © Benoit Tessier/Reuters/Corbis **219** © PA Photos/TopFoto **220** © Vittoriano Rastelli/ Corbis **221** © Toni Thorimbert/Sygma/Corbis **222** Photoshot **223** © Anthea Simms **224** Chinsee George and Iannaccone Thomas/Condé Nast Publications **226–27** © Ullsteinbild/Topfoto **228** © Baril/Roncen/Corbis KIPA **229** © Frederic Meylan/Sygma/Corbis **230** © Ullsteinbild/TopFoto **231** © STR New/Reuters/ Reuters/Corbis **232** © Pierre Vauthey/Sygma/ Corbis **233** Jean-Claude Deutsch/Paris Match via Getty Images **234T**, **234B** akg-images/E. Mierendorff **235T** Gerard Julien/AFP/Getty Images **235B** © RA/Lebrecht Music & Arts **236** © Jermaine Francis/Outline/Corbis **237** © dpa picture alliance/Alamy **238** Giuseppe Cacace/ AFP/Getty Images **239T** Pierre Verdy/AFP/ Getty Images **239B** Photo of Prada black Saffiano courtesy of Prada **240** catwalking.com **241** akg-images/Mondadori Portfolio/Nino Leto **242**, **243** © Anthea Simms **244** Pierre Guillaud/ AFP/Getty Images **245** © Julio Donoso/Sygma/ Corbis **246** © Roger-Viollet/TopFoto **247** Sipa Press/REX **248** Topham/AP **249** © Eric Fougere/Kipa/Corbis **250T** catwalking.com **250B** Bukajlo Frederic/Sipa/Rex **251** Antonio de Moraes Barros Filho/Getty Images **252** catwalking.com **253** © Elfie Semotan **254** © Anthea Simms **255TL** Associated Newspapers/ Rex **255BL** Rex Features **255R** Doug Kanter/ AFP/Getty Images **256** catwalking.com **257** Rex Features **258**, **259T**, **259B** catwalking.com **260** © Ronald Stoops **262** © Kerry Taylor Auctions **263** Pierre Verdy/AFP/Getty Images **264** Camera Press/Figarophoto/Alexandre Weinberger **265** © Elizabeth Broekaert **266** Pierre Verdy/AFP/Getty Images **267T** Francois Guillot/AFP/Getty Images **267B** © Anthea Simms **268** © Giampaolo Sgura/Trunk Archive **269** akg-images/Mondadori Portfolio **270T** Ken Towner/Associated Newspapers/REX **270B** © Vittoriano Rastelli/Corbis **271** © Janet Mayer/ Splash News/Corbis **272** Francois Guillot /AFP/ Getty Images **273** © epa european pressphoto agency b.v./Alamy **274TL**, **274TR**, **274B** catwalking.com **275** Rex Features **276** © Stefano Rellandini/Reuters **277** © Piero Cruciatti/Alamy **278** catwalking.com **279T**, **279B**, **280** © Anthea Simms **281** Photo by Kurita Kaku/Gamma-Rapho via Getty Images **282L**, **282R** © Anthea Simms **283** © firstVIEW **284** Bukajlo Frederic/Sipa/Rex **285** Sipa Press/Rex Features **286** © Fairchild Photo Service/Condé Nast/Corbis **287** Ericksen Kyle/Condé Nast Publications **288** Terence Donovan Archive/Getty Images **289** © Evan Hurd/Corbis **290T** © Anthea Simms **290B** Gareth Cattermole/Getty Images **291** © Anthea Simms **292** © David Slijper/Trunk Archive **293** Matt Baron/BEI/Rex **294** © Charles Platiau/ Reuters/Corbis **295** catwalking.com **296** Giovanni Giannoni/Condé Nast Publications **297** Courtesy of Alexander McQueen **298T** Sipa Press/Rex **298B** Eric Ryan/Getty Images **299** Nicolas Asfouri/AFP/Getty Images **300** Francois Guillot/AFP/Getty Images **301** Philip Hollis/Rex **302TL**, **302TR** Yoshikazu Tsuno/AFP/Getty Images **302B** Hugo Philpott/AFP/Getty Images **303** Photograph by Richard Stonehouse, Camera Press, London **304** Derek Mossop/Rex **305** akg-images/picture-alliance/Agence Zeppelin **306** Dimitrios Kambouris/Getty Images for MAC **307T** Suzanne Plunkett/Bloomberg News/Getty Images **307BL** Camera Press/Anthea Simms **307BR** © PA Photos/TopFoto

Acknowledgements

With heartfelt thanks to my friends for their support, words of wisdom, generosity, hospitality, and above all for their sense of humour.

Author Biography

Linda Watson graduated from Northumbria University with a double first in Fashion Design and Historical Studies. She has worked with three of the fashion visionaries featured in this book – Vivienne Westwood, Celia Birtwell and the late Jean Muir. A former fashion writer for British *Vogue* and contributor to *The Independent*, she is the author of *Vogue Twentieth Century Fashion* and *Vogue on Vivienne Westwood*. Linda is currently Reader in Fashion at Northumbria University.

Thierry Hermès / Charles Frederick Worth / Thomas Burberry / Jeanne Lanvin / Mariano Fortuny / Madeleine Vionnet / Paul Poiret / Guccio Gucci / Gabrielle Chanel Elsa Schiaparelli / Mainbocher / Cristóbal Balenciaga Salvatore Ferragamo / Norman Norell / Norman Hartnell Madame Grès / Christian Dior / Claire McCardell / Charles James / Roger Vivier / Jacques Fath / Pierre Balmain Emilio Pucci / Ottavio & Rosita Missoni / Pierre Cardin Rudi Gernreich / André Courrèges / Hubert de Givenchy Geoffrey Beene / Jean Muir / Sonia Rykiel / Oscar de la Renta / Halston / Valentino Garavani / Emanuel Ungaro Giorgio Armani / Mary Quant / Karl Lagerfeld / Barbara Hulanicki / Yves Saint Laurent / Issey Miyake / Kenzo Takada / Ralph Lauren / Azzedine Alaïa / Vivienne Westwood / Rei Kawakubo / Calvin Klein / Ossie Clark Jil Sander / Tommy Nutter / Yohji Yamamoto / Kansai Yamamoto / Paul Smith / Gianni Versace / Donna Karan Thierry Mugler / Claude Montana / Miuccia Prada / Franco Moschino / Christian Lacroix / Jean Paul Gaultier / Helmut Lang / Stephen Jones / Martin Margiela / Dries Van Noten / Domenico Dolce & Stefano Gabbana / John Galliano / Tom Ford / Junya Watanabe / Marc Jacobs Philip Treacy / Hedi Slimane / Alexander McQueen Hussein Chalayan / Gareth P

US$40.00

ISBN 978-1-78067-578-7

04000

9 781780 675787

www.laurenceking.com